Pet Whisperer

Pet Whisperer

My Life as an Animal Healer

SARAH-JANE LE BLANC

POCKET
BOOKS
LONDON • SYDNEY • NEW YORK • TORONTO

First published in Great Britain by Pocket Books, 2010
A division of Simon & Schuster UK Ltd
A CBS Company

1 3 5 7 9 10 8 6 4 2

Simon & Schuster UK Ltd
1st Floor
222 Gray's Inn Road
London WC1X 8HB

www.simonandschuster.co.uk

Simon & Schuster Australia
Sydney

A CIP catalogue record for this book is available
from the British Library.

ISBN: 978-1-84983-085-0

Typeset by Hewer Text UK Ltd, Edinburgh
Printed and Bound in Great Britain by
CPI Cox & Wyman, Reading, Berkshire RG1 8EX

This book is dedicated with deepest love and gratitude to those who mean so much to me.

To Derek, my husband to be, who supports me on every level, gives me boundless love and encouragement, shows unfailing faith in me, keeps me on my path and ensures that my feet are always firmly on the ground. Thank you from the bottom of my heart. LTCS – always.

To my children, who just wanted me to be happy. Nathan, who, in the early days, was embarrassed about what I do yet quietly and without complaint endured the school-ground talk after each media exposure (not to mention the barking and meowing he received on the football pitch!), and India, who has a child's unconditional, unashamed pride and faith in her mother and actively encouraged me, displaying unshakable belief in my abilities when my confidence was low and my self-doubt high.

To my mum, Morag, my sister, Samantha, my brother-in-law, Darren, and my nephews, Cameron and Ramsay, who have all stood by me and supported me and encouraged me as I made the sometimes difficult and often challenging metamorphosis from a 'normal' person into someone who communicates with animals on a daily basis!

And, of course, to all the animals – especially Dan and Barney – without them, this book would not exist and I would not be the person I am today. *Thank you* doesn't seem enough.

Contents

Acknowledgements

There are many people to thank for this book – I'm sure I'll forget someone, as it's such an exciting time, so, for that, my apologies!

On my journey I have been supported by a great many people – my clients, students, teachers, friends and family – and, of course, the animals. Without them and many others this book could not have been written. I would like to express specific thanks to:

Linda Watson-Brown for lovingly nurturing this book from conception to completion with such enthusiasm, commitment and integrity.

Clare Hulton for all her hard work, skill and expertise behind the scenes, which made this book a reality.

Kerri Sharp and the team at Simon & Schuster, who have been fantastic. Everything they have come up with has enhanced the book beyond my wildest dreams. They have made all of this seem so easy and I appreciate their approach with a novice such as myself!

Amelia Kinkade, who taught me so much while inspiring me to fearlessly embrace my new-found learning and the animal kingdom that awaited me.

I would truly like to thank everyone who has entrusted their beloved animal companions to me. Without your belief and faith in me, I wouldn't have been able to make a difference. Each of you has enhanced my journey by teaching me with your feedback – thank you for being a part of it.

Finally, my deepest, heartfelt thanks to our amazing animal friends who have so much to teach us; words fail to express my eternal gratitude and awe to those wonderful beings in the animal kingdom who have taught me so much along the way on my wonderful journey of discovery and exploration. From you I have learned the most and it has been both an absolute privilege and an honour to serve you.

I'm looking forward to the next part of my journey – I know I will meet many new friends and teachers along the way . . .

Prologue

Flying

I stood in the bathroom of my house and watched as a beautiful red admiral butterfly beat its fragile wings against the window.

Night was beginning to fall, but the last rays of sunshine were flooding through the glass and illuminating the stunning pattern of the creature's body. It was becoming more and more frantic. It had clearly been trapped for some time, as it seemed to be panicking, flapping its wings harder and harder. I wondered how long it could keep going and moved closer to the window. I thought that maybe I could reach my hand up slowly to open it without scaring the butterfly away, but it was too high for me to even reach. The butterfly seemed unable to recognize where the escape route was, perhaps having worked itself into such a frenzy trying to get out that it could no longer tell where freedom lay.

'Can you help it, Mum?' asked the voice beside me. My six-year-old daughter had crept quietly into the room. Her question wasn't the usual one of a child wanting the parent to make things better – there was something else to what India was asking. 'Can you talk to it?' she whispered.

I dragged my eyes from the butterfly and looked into my daughter's face. I smiled. 'Maybe,' I said. 'Maybe. I'll try.'

I did what I'd taught myself to do and emptied my mind. I relaxed my body and made sure I was as grounded as possible – and tried to not let myself think about the fact that I was going to try to communicate with a butterfly. And then . . . how can I explain it? I sent my thoughts to the exquisite creature pounding its body into the glass. I asked it to come to me. I said that I would take it to safety. I explained that I was going to stretch out my arm, hold out my hand and wait for it to fly across and settle on me. Then, my mind whispered, I would walk along the hall-way to another room where I could open a window fully and let it fly out into the garden.

I did exactly what I had promised.

I stretched out my arm.

I held out my hand.

I waited.

Nothing happened.

I waited a little longer, trying to send thoughts of love and assistance to the creature who was still pounding against the window.

Still nothing.

I was disappointed, but not completely surprised. Who could really have thought it would have worked? I smiled softly at India, sorry that I couldn't do what she'd wanted. 'Look, Mum,' she whispered. 'Look!' The butterfly had gone completely still and my heart sank – had it died? Had it finally had to give up? I felt a jump in my heart but there was no sense of sadness or loss – what was going on? Seconds later, the butterfly stretched out its wings. Calmly, peacefully and with the most beautiful grace, it flew over to me and very softly settled on my still-outstretched hand. Keeping my hand flat, I did exactly as I promised and walked along the hallway towards a bedroom at the end of my house where a large picture window opened out on to the garden below. The butterfly didn't move when I got there and I realized it was waiting for something. 'Go,' I whispered. It opened up its wings fully and took to flight, hovering outside for a moment, almost as if to give me the opportunity to see its full splendour.

As I stood there in the empty room, I laughed quietly to myself. I had just communicated, by thought alone, with a butterfly. How mad was that? I couldn't help wonder. How had my life come to this – how had I become a real-life Dr Dolittle who spoke with animals on a daily basis?

Well, it had all started with a dog called Dan . . .

Chapter 1

A Special Visitor

I have always been a very pragmatic person. I like to think things through. I like when there are solutions to problems and when things work out in a rational way. Six years ago, I was living a sensible life. I was a married mother of two with a long-term career in community education, and my world was a level-headed, ordinary affair – until one night when everything got turned upside down.

My normal bedtime routine was just the same that evening as any other. After reading a few chapters of a book to relax, I flipped the light out and snuggled under the duvet. As soon as I did, an image of a dog popped into my head.

Dan.

As the image appeared, so did the name. I wasn't asleep – it had been only seconds since I'd stopped reading – and I wasn't letting my mind wander. It was as if a fully formed moving portrait of a brown and white collie had just pushed itself into my brain at the same time as I heard the name *Dan*. It was so clear, so picture perfect, that I was totally taken aback. I didn't know anyone with a dog like that; I didn't know anyone – man or beast – called Dan, so I had absolutely no idea why such a thought would materialize, but I didn't think too much about it. 'Get to sleep,' I told myself, 'you're clearly exhausted if you're imagining stuff.' The next morning, I briefly remembered what had happened but it didn't prey on my mind.

The following night, it happened again. I read a little of my book, turned the light off, settled into bed, and 'Dan' reappeared. As before, it was odd, but I wondered whether I was simply subconsciously replaying the previous evening. I ignored it and went to sleep.

When the same dog came back into my head under the same circumstances for the third night in a row, I had to think again. I knew I wasn't asleep – I knew that I hadn't been asleep any of the three nights it had happened. I hadn't been dreaming, my mind hadn't been playing tricks on me; I was wide awake, but, for some reason, this image of an earnest, beautiful, unusually coloured collie was coming back time after time and telling me *Dan, Dan, Dan* on each occasion.

My pragmatic side came into play. I knew nothing about animals so I had to think laterally.

At that time, I was a Youth Project Manager. If a member of staff said to me that a teenager had come up to them at youth club on three consecutive occasions, I'd ask what their response had been. If they said they'd done nothing, I'd be furious. I would advise my staff that the young person had come to them because they obviously felt a connection or felt they could help them, so why ignore them? Maybe I should apply the same logic to this dog that wouldn't leave me alone.

I thought, *This is happening for a reason*. Even though I had no idea what that reason was, I decided to go with it – out of curiosity as much as anything else. I simply formed the thought in my head and sent it by silently saying: *Do you want to talk to me?*

Now, there may be many people reading this book who have already experienced animal communication; they themselves may be psychic or know someone who is. There may be those who have gone through beautiful, remarkable encounters with our animal friends. But there may also be those who have never come across such a thing. I was firmly in the latter camp. I had never been touched by anything like this before and I certainly wasn't prepared for the collie's response.

Do you want to talk to me? I asked.

Duh! came the reply.

I was dealing with a stroppy canine teenager!

The voice which came back was full of attitude, almost as if he was saying, *I wondered how long it would take you.* I wasn't prepared for any of this, but I undoubtedly couldn't have imagined such bearing from a creature that was in my head. I didn't expect this dog to actually speak back to me and I certainly didn't expect it to be so sassy. However, I did have to wonder whether that was what had happened – had we been 'talking'? None of the words between us had been voiced out loud. I didn't know what was going on and I didn't really expect anything because, basically, I didn't know that this could happen to people. I knew nothing about animal communication. In fact, at that moment in time, I thought I was very close to a heart attack. My heartbeat was racing, my pulse was pounding, I was sweating and confused.

My youth-worker side kicked in again and I thought the best thing to do would be to just treat the situation like one in which a teenager needed something from me. I started asking the dog non-invasive questions, such as *Where do you live?* but I didn't get any more words back. I knew that he was the one called Dan, that he wasn't referring to someone else, but I soon realized that this situation wasn't the same as having a dialogue with another person. I was asking questions but the information that he was giving back to me was coming in the form of pictures.

I'm not even sure if I can describe how bizarre this process felt. I wasn't lying there saying things out loud in a doggy voice, barking to myself or hallucinating! All that was happening – and what still happens – is that I was 'sending' questions to the image in my head and receiving images back again, almost instantaneously. Very quickly, Dan sent me pictures of a family. The sense of loss was completely tangible – there was a woman, and I felt that there was a male presence around (although I didn't see a picture of a man) and lots of children. Actually, I got the strong feeling that there were too many children, and

I somehow knew that feeling was coming from Dan's perspective.

Suddenly, things changed. From this dog with attitude who had almost reprimanded me for taking so long to reciprocate contact, I felt an overwhelming sense of loss and sadness. These were emotions which came through to me very strongly and which I easily recognized – as anyone would – it took no special talent. Immediately the image of a little boy was given to me, with the name *Jamie*. Again, without quite knowing why or how, I felt that the children Dan had shown me were quite rough with him, and he didn't like that at all. Jamie was different, gentle, and Dan loved the way they had been together.

Had been.

There was a huge sense of loss and grief, and I realized that everything to do with Jamie was in the past for Dan. I believed that they were no longer together and he missed the child dreadfully. I was confused. This dog seemed to be with a big family but he had a sense of loss around the one child. As I was thinking through all of this information I felt that Dan had tummy pains, because he kept pulling my focus towards his stomach, and I knew, instinctively, that he was quite poorly. I had a really strong feeling that it was to do with food rather than anything more medical. I asked if it hurt when he ate and he said *Yes*, so I knew my suspicion was right. I didn't know how I knew these things and I wasn't thinking it all out, I was simply 'going with the flow' and following my intuition.

My view of Dan was changing – his feelings about the little boy called Jamie and the pain he was in made me think that he was actually a really unhappy dog and not the cheeky creature with attitude who had first spoken back to me. As well as his very real sense of unhappiness and loneliness there was a feeling of being completely misunderstood. I felt drawn to the throat area, which felt very dry and constricted, as if he quite literally couldn't voice what it was that was going on. The emotional build-up was huge. He really felt like a grief-stricken animal, unhappy and unheard. I asked Dan where Jamie had gone. He didn't give me an answer in a conversational sense, but I got the sense that the boy had moved, or that someone had moved, and I saw Dan then with another woman and a man. I couldn't have identified them if the police had shown me a line-up, though – they were faceless figures that simply symbolized a man and a woman.

I felt that I had to interpret all I had been sent. Dan seemed to have left his family, or been taken from them, and he was now living with a man and a woman. It wasn't that he was unhappy there – I knew he'd been unhappy with all those children – but there was still loss about leaving his other family and there was something going on with his new home that made him unhappy.

I still find it hard to express how this all affected me. I wasn't someone who worked with animals, and I wasn't someone who had previous experience of psychic connections, but what had happened that night (and the shock I'd had when Dan had appeared previously) was actually feeling quite natural. I didn't feel mad; I was just lying in my bed getting all this information and not really knowing how to process it. I was simply absorbing it, going with it and waiting to see where it took me. It suddenly occurred to me that I could almost deflect Dan from the pain and grief he was feeling by putting a 'normal' question to him. *Do you have a favourite walk?* I asked him. Quick as a flash, his response came back. *Do you have a favourite walk?* I nearly jumped out of my skin! I hadn't expected him to ask me something. I didn't know they answered back. I thought I did the talking. I thought I was in control, the one who was shaping it and leading it – but then again, I didn't actually know anything about this whole business. I said, *Yes, I do have a favourite walk*, and tried to send back a picture of a path beside a river that I liked. I felt a surge of appreciation.

This seemed like a good place to end our communication so I asked Dan if there was anything he needed. He replied that he wanted healing work and that was one thing which did make sense to me. Over the past few years, while involved in my community-education work, I had been successful in introducing clients to complementary therapies, often with incredible results, especially where drug users and highly stressed client groups were involved. Some of them had experienced reiki and crystal therapy, and I remembered that there had been one lady who had talked about how different colours symbolized different things, and that some people believed that emotions could be affected by colours. I'd been learning about all of this myself and practising a little bit of healing work with my family, and I saw no reason I couldn't apply that to Dan – after all, it wasn't as if I had a rule book to guide me through all of this. I dug deep into my memory and tried to dredge up what this lady had taught my clients – luckily, I remembered. I sent him lots of love wrapped in a cannonball of pink light, which I was pretty sure was the colour of love. He immediately replied: *Eeurgh*! The stroppy teenager was back, and he didn't like his masculinity being threatened by such a girly colour, no matter how much it was sent with the best intentions and may have helped him. I sent some blue instead, which I'd remembered is a healing colour, and some yellow, which I thought was related to helping tummy problems.

As I was closing off and saying goodbye to Dan, I said to him that I didn't know where he lived or what I could really do for him. I apologized and assured him I would do my best to try and find him. As soon as I sent the message, I got a blinding headache. I never get headaches so I knew that it wasn't mine, it was his. It was an instant pain to the head, which thankfully was only temporary. It was as if Dan had just flashed it to me and then it went. I felt very much that it was significant, much more so than just a headache, so to speak. I also had a sense that the headache didn't belong to him, it belonged to the female guardian, his 'mum', but I had no idea what made me intuit things that way; I just knew it was important.

We'd been communicating just short of an hour by that time and by the time Dan left, I was exhausted. Although I'd felt calmer as our time had gone on, I was now agitated again. I sat up in bed, put the light on and grabbed a notepad. I wrote down everything that had happened, every message I'd received, every interpretation I'd made.

I thought I was losing my mind.

It was beyond my realm of experience but I knew that I wasn't sleeping, that this had actually happened. Although I did have all those irrational, speedy thoughts flying through my head, I also had a very assured sense of *this is happening for a reason*. I needed to go with it and not be scared of it - even though I was terrified.

I finally fell asleep, not knowing that my life would never be the same again.

Chapter 2

A Whole New World

The next morning, my head was still buzzing with everything that had happened. I knew that I had to confide in someone, even if I wasn't quite sure what I was going to say, so I called my close friend Mary and arranged to meet her for coffee. 'I've got something to tell you,' I began, 'and I really need you to just listen and not respond or interrupt until I've got it all out. Don't laugh either.'

Poor Mary – she probably thought I was going to tell her I was pregnant or changing jobs; I very much doubt that she expected one of her best friends to say that she had started talking to animals!

Mary did just what I asked and listened to the whole story. When I'd finished, she reached across the table and took my hand, her face solemn. 'Sarah-Jane,' she said, 'you can't tell anyone about this.'

It wasn't the response I'd expected. 'What? Why not?' I asked.

'Talking to animals? People will think you're mad, love. It wasn't that long ago women were being burned at the stake as witches for less.'

'I don't know what to do, Mary. I'm sure that this has happened because I'm meant to do something; I just don't know what.'

'I'm telling you exactly what to do,' she answered firmly. 'Nothing. Keep quiet. You'll forget about it ... hopefully. It was probably just a dream anyway.'

I knew she was wrong. It wasn't a dream, and I was sure that I was not meant to ignore it. I went back home and got straight on the computer – I needed to do something practical. I'd needed to offload, get it off my chest, and now I wanted information. Had anyone else been through this? I wondered. Had anyone else had the same experience? My boundaries of understanding and conception were quite broad, I was open to most things and thought that the world was a far more intriguing place than the sum total of the things we had discovered so far, but, despite all this, I still had the feeling that this particular experience of mine was very, very odd indeed. That morning I had needed to verbalize it; I'd needed to share it and get a reaction, to see what someone else's attitude was – from Mary, I'd got only fear and concern. She was speaking from a caring place, and she did seem to be worried about me, but I was actually quite calm and believed that all I needed to do was work all of this out logically and it would make sense.

All I could think to google was 'talking to animals' – I didn't know any of the terminology at that stage, and I don't think I even thought of it as a 'psychic' link. The search engine threw up more results than I would have expected but there was one name that came up first and was repeated throughout the pages – *Amelia Kinkade*. It turned out that this lady was based in America and was already becoming internationally recognized for the amazing work she was doing with animals. What I read made sense. There were other people who had similar experiences and they were actually being recognized for what they were doing, rather than run out of town – maybe I wasn't going to be burned at the stake just yet.

The website said that Amelia was going to be visiting the Lake District to lead an animal communication work-shop that very weekend – only two days away. Places were limited and would fill very quickly, according to what I was reading – and the information had been up for a while. There was a contact number that I rang straight away, only to be told that there was one place left because there had been a cancellation – it felt like that place was meant for me, that it had my name written all over it. I booked immediately. It was my daughter India's birth-day the day I was planning to leave, so it was going to be hectic, but I genuinely felt that this would provide me with some answers. Until then, I planned to just carry on as normal – which meant doing some chores then taking my puppy, Lady, to her dog-training class that night.

I had been to one session before; the woman who ran the class brought her old dog with her to demonstrate what we had to do. That night she was showing us a new training command and my mind was wandering a bit because of all that had happened – until I heard the words, 'for example, my dog Dan . . .'

I stumbled through the rest of the hour, my mind in a whirl – the room was spinning and I was having trouble breathing. As soon as she said *Dan*, I knew she meant *my* Dan, the dog who had come to me. There was no doubt in my mind, but how on earth was I going to tell her? How the hell was I going to say to that woman that her dog had been coming to me at night and talking to me?

After the class there were a busy few minutes with people wanting to chat to the instructor and the next group coming in, during which I just bit the bullet and asked her if there was any way we could meet for a chat soon. 'Yes,' she said, 'are you worried about Lady?' I took a deep breath. 'No, actually – it's about Dan.' To my amazement, and her credit, she didn't ask why I wanted to talk about her dog, a dog that I didn't know and had never met, she just said, 'OK, meet me on Friday, as I finish work early.'

So much was going to happen on one day – I had India's birthday party to organize and hold before heading off to the weekend workshop in the Lake District, and now I was faced with finding out just what had really happened when I had 'spoken' to Dan. My head was full of questions. Had I really been communicating with this woman's dog? Had I picked up on anything that was accurate? What was she going to make of what I would tell her? My real fear was that she would think I was mad.

When I got home from class there was a message waiting on my answering machine. A few weeks earlier I had mentioned to some friends the complementary therapies that my clients had found so useful, and that I'd been practising healing work with my family. I'd got chatting to one woman who I didn't really know, Gloria, and she'd asked if that sort of thing ever worked with animals and whether I could do it. At the time I'd said no, laughing that I wouldn't know where to start. She had mentioned that she had a horse, Maple, who she was worried about; she'd said she really wanted to try some complementary therapies with her, but I'd brushed her off. It was her voice on the machine, asking again if I'd consider working with her horse – even though I had never for a moment suggested that I was in that line of business at all. In fact, I didn't even know that such a line of business existed!

After the events of the previous few days, I was seriously starting to wonder whether I was receiving a series of messages, all pushing me in the same direction. If that was the case, then I needed to be open to anything that came my way. I called Gloria back and said I'd visit her and her horse the next day, but I had no idea what would happen or what I would be doing. I also made a conscious decision not to do any more research on animal communication. I would go into my meeting with Maple with an open mind, free of anything I'd read elsewhere, but also with an awareness that I was testing this gift which had appeared from nowhere.

When I met with Gloria I told her that I needed a few

details, such as what she wanted me to look out for, but I didn't want a full history. I hoped that Maple, like Dan, would tell me what she wanted me to hear – if anything. It turned out that since we first met, when Gloria had mentioned her concerns about the horse's behaviour, Maple had actually had an accident. The previous day, she had torn a ligament and had to be stabled awaiting the vet's visit and confirmation of the diagnosis. Maple was incredibly agitated and distressed, and Gloria had called me in desperation because she was trying to escape from the stable. Gloria was willing to try anything.

This was very challenging for me, as I was going into a situation in which I knew I would be scared. I had no experience of horses and I found their sheer size terrifying. If I could get anything, any message from Maple through my own wall of fear, I'd be very surprised. I visited the stable immediately and found an incredibly distraught horse who was clearly as anxious as I was. She was trying so hard to escape that I could barely get in. She was also pawing at the ground and pacing around in a very agitated manner, trying to barge past me.

My heart was pounding and I felt fear like I had never experienced in my entire life – I desperately needed to get out of that stable. The drive and panic to flee was immense, and physically and emotionally consuming. I had to use all of my reserves to keep my feet on the ground and ignore the screaming in my head – 'Get out! Get out! Run!' I felt that my heart was going to burst through my skin, I had a cold sweat down my back and, according to those watching, my face was as white as a sheet. I assumed that I was frightened of Maple, which made sense, but I also felt that there was something else going on. I could have walked out – I knew that I had an escape route – yet I felt pure terror. Maple was already scared and would be picking up on what I was feeling, so I needed to calm down before I could work with her. I centred myself and tried to push the fear aside.

My growing interest in healing work had led me to various workshops and I had recently started a diploma course in healing work, so I started some grounding work on Maple, as well as working directly on her injured leg. As I worked, it was evident that her terror remained one of the main problems – she'd cause himself further damage if she kept trying to get out – and therefore the primary focus of the session was to reduce her fear. After a while she visibly started to relax, but my own fear was still present and my heart continued to pound – although admittedly not quite as violently as it had to begin with. As we continued to work together, we both calmed down a bit more and I was able to perform more healing on her leg. This involved me clearing the blocked energy at the site of the injury, sending images of healing colours to Maple over a period of about twenty minutes, and channelling healing energies through my body to her. Clearing the blockages from Maple's energy system allowed the energy to flow freely around her body, activating her body's capacity to self-heal.

Despite feeling somewhat calmer after I had done my work, I was hugely relieved to leave that stable. I wrapped Maple in loving, healing energies at the end of the session and left. I told Gloria that I had done what I could, and asked her to let me know how the horse was over the next couple of days.

I revisited the events of the meeting in my head all night long. Yes, I had been frightened of animals all my life; yes, horses were big and scary when they weren't standing still; yes, it made sense that enclosed in a small space with a distressed and agitated horse anyone would be scared; and, yes, my fear would increase Maple's fear. But still, I just knew that my terror of the situation did not amount to what I had experienced in that stable. I had felt claustrophobic, my heart had been pounding, but the worst aspect had been the screaming alarm bells of danger and panic in my head simultaneously accompanied by my whole body willing me, driving me, to flee. My adrenaline had been pumping and every ounce of my being had been on full alert, ready to run.

As if a light switch had been flipped, I suddenly realized what it was – it was Maple's alarm I had felt, not my own.

She was a field horse, never usually stabled, which would naturally make her feel claustrophobic. I had been experiencing the flight reaction, where my body – feeling what she felt – had gone into full alert with an overwhelming need to run. Poor Maple. Everything that I had felt had been her pain, her fear, her panic, and it was awful. I quickly rang Gloria and told her what I believed. She confirmed that Maple had never been in an enclosed space before, so I advised her to reassure the horse, every day, by telling her how much longer she would be in the stable, so that she knew she wasn't going to be there forever. I suggested that she explain time in terms of 'dark nights' so that Maple would more easily understand and recognize when another day had passed. I told Gloria to talk to her, explain to her what was happening, so that she could be constantly aware of what was going on and why.

The next morning, Gloria rang me to say that she and the others at the yard couldn't believe the change in Maple. After we had spoken, she had spent ages with her horse, continuously explaining things to her and reassuring her that she would soon be back in the field with the others as soon as a certain number of dark nights had passed. This was all very helpful for me, as I hadn't really known what I was doing, and had only patched together bits of knowledge and information from lots of areas I'd dipped my toe in. Thankfully it had worked and I had to wonder whether this was yet another sign that things were simply meant to be.

I was delighted at this whole new world which had opened up to me, but I knew that I had something much bigger ahead of me – this was the day that I was going to meet with Dan's guardian.

Chapter 3

Opening the Door

I met with Dan's guardian, Kairyn, the next day. I was very nervous about telling her what had happened – partly because it all still seemed a bit mad to me, and partly because, in training classes, she was very brisk and no-nonsense. Although when I'd first raised the subject she had been quick to accept that I wanted to talk about her dog, she didn't really know what I was going to come out with – and neither did I. This was all new to both of us. It transpired that, outside the training environment, Kairyn was actually a very warm person, and I just launched straight into what I needed to say.

'I have to get all of this out, Kairyn,' I said by way of a warning. 'Can you just listen to it and not judge me or think I'm crazy until you've heard it all, please?' I think she was a little bemused – who wouldn't be? – but also intrigued, so she just sat there at my kitchen table, while I spilled it all out. 'I know this is all unusual, to say the least,' I began, 'and I can't really explain it to you – I can't really explain it to myself – but I believe that I've been communicating with Dan.'

There.

I'd said it and the world hadn't crashed in and she hadn't started laughing – it was out there, and now I needed to follow up on my part of the bargain. Kairyn wasn't interrupting, she wasn't leaving or in hysterics, so all I had to do was tell her all I knew about a dog I'd never met. I went through what had happened, giving her every piece of information that had been sent to me by Dan, and finished by saying that I was leaving later that day to go to a weekend workshop on animal communication and could hopefully give her some more answers when I got back.

I waited as Kairyn sat there. She didn't look shocked, and nor did she look as if she was about to call the men in white coats to take me away – then she verified everything, every single word I'd said.

'It's all true, Sarah-Jane. Every little thing you've told me about Dan – what he looks like, how he behaves, what his background was – you've got every little thing spot-on. I have no idea what's happening, but you know everything there is to know about my dog.'

She told me that Dan had been removed from a very large family with lots of children. He hadn't been treated particularly well, not because they didn't love him or had been deliberately cruel to him, but that it was just the wrong environment for the type of dog Dan was. He was quite a nervous creature and so many children in one place had been too much for him. Kairyn knew that he had come from a large family, and recognized that he was pining for someone despite ultimately being better off out of it.

Kairyn said that she had been having some problems with Dan and felt that they were due to his previous home life – perhaps he was still unsettled, or perhaps he felt scared that things could go back to that way of living which was not what he wanted, and he was certainly defensive. She said that she felt it was nervous aggression; he hadn't bitten anyone, but that was because of her expertise as a trainer and the fact that she could read the signs in advance before he had the chance to act. Kairyn had to be very careful with Dan and I knew that this was the nervousness and anxiety I'd picked up on. However, I felt there was more to it than the life he had come from and the fact that he may have been feeling unsettled. This was my first real experience of animal communication and I was being thrown in at the deep end – I realized very quickly that it isn't all about the animal and me, it's about the guardian as well. What Dan had shown to me was a home environment in which there were some difficulties and that is something that I now find to be a very common experience. Animals pick up on, and mirror, what is going on with their guardians and I now had to ask Kairyn some very personal questions.

I asked whether Dan had problems with his stomach, which Kairyn again verified immediately. In fact, she said he was due to go to the vet for a biopsy soon to find out exactly what was going on. As soon as she said it I just knew this was wrong – a feeling of fear washed over me. Dan didn't want this to happen and he didn't need it to happen. I realize now that I don't have to be sitting with an animal, or a photograph to get a connection with an animal. On this occasion, my connection with Dan was tangible as Kairyn and I spoke across the kitchen table.

'No!' I said, emotionally, as I felt his worry in my own body. 'That's not to happen! He's not meant to go for a biopsy, Kairyn.'

'Why not?' she asked. 'I need to find out what's wrong with him, whether there's something physical behind how he is. This can happen – sometimes a dog will act out aggression or other behaviours because he's unwell. I have to rule that out, Sarah-Jane, and I can't risk him becoming vicious.'

My dilemma was that I somehow knew Dan's issues were to do with Kairyn more than himself. I had to be sensitive. 'OK, I understand, but do you mind me asking you a few things?' Kairyn nodded that I should go ahead. 'Do you have stomach problems?' I don't know why I asked that specific question, as I knew nothing about what I was doing then – though I'm now aware that it was completely appropriate and the right question to ask. Kairyn looked puzzled, but admitted that she couldn't tolerate wheat, among other things, and that she had terrible problems with bloating. I said that I couldn't go against any vet's decision but that I felt very strongly that she needed to sort out her own stomach problems in order to help Dan, who would then sort himself out. I now know that a lot of animals mirror their human guardian's health issues, but

I've also discovered that many people will happily spend lots of time, energy and money looking into their pet's health problems but not their own.

These days I know that once I've made the initial communication with an animal, that line of communication has been opened; it's like a gate has been unlocked, and I no longer need a photograph to hand or a meeting with the animal. I've found on some occasions that an animal I've been doing communication work with has just popped in and said '*Hello!*' when I've been doing something completely mundane around the house – sometimes they don't need to be asked or welcomed or sought out; they just like to keep in touch. Nowadays, when people call me to ask about work with their animals, it's often the case that I can do the work even before I get a picture, because the person I'm speaking to is already thinking about their animal and I can tap into their link and connection with their animal immediately. When someone is concentrating so intently on their animal, all I'm doing is hooking into the connection they've established. I didn't understand it at this early stage, but this was already happening with Kairyn and her dog – Dan's feelings were flowing for me. Sometimes I can be speaking to someone for an hour but don't get any idea of what the animal looks like, or sometimes it's just a sensation such as a small dog, large dog, wiry dog, long-haired dog. I was doing it unconsciously then, whereas now I do it consciously. I was picking up on the connection that

Kairyn had with Dan, talking about him and being concerned about his operation. It was a box-of-hankies job for both of us!

I sensed that Kairyn needed to work on herself too, which brought me on to the very difficult issue of how Dan got on with her partner. Animals don't really have a filter. If they are happy to talk, they will tell you what you need to know, or what they think you need to know, and then it's all out in the open. That can be problematic. I've spent many a sleepless night worrying over how exactly I'm going to raise certain topics with people, and with Kairyn this was the dilemma I faced. Dan had basically told me that he didn't like Kairyn's partner and that he thought she shouldn't be with him – in fact, he'd told me that she could do better. I knew that if Kairyn said her relationship was great then I would just have to leave it, despite Dan's frustration. However, when I asked how her partner and dog got on, she said, 'They don't.'

Her partner felt that she spent too much time with the dogs and it was a constant source of friction between them. I told Kairyn that I'd had a terrible headache when I'd last spoken with Dan and said that I thought it was maybe hers. She asked what time this had happened and got tearful again when I told her it was at half past eleven. She said that at that time she'd had a horrendous fight with her partner, taken the dogs and left the house. I told her that Dan had sent that headache to me to prove to her that genuine communication had taken place and that he needed some healing work for his fear and anger, which I did do at a later date – and, yes, I did meet Dan at that point too.

As I finished my session with Kairyn, I knew that the door had been opened for me to enter an amazing new world that I hadn't even known existed until a few days earlier. Dan had shown me an incredible opportunity and, despite feeling incredibly nervous and more than a little scared, I was going to seize this chance to make some sense of my life and things that I knew nothing of.

I bustled around the house getting everything ready for India's birthday party, with one eye on the suitcase that was waiting for me at the front door. In a few hours, I'd be in my car on the way to meeting the woman who had shown the world just how miraculous our relationships with animals could be – and my life would change almost beyond recognition.

Chapter 4

Believing in Myself

I drove to the Lake District with my head buzzing and on a real high from what I'd just experienced with Kairyn. I was going into a situation where I was the new girl, but I still felt a positive glow throughout my mind and body. To this day, I always say in my own workshops that I know how people feel when they are taking their first steps on this amazing journey and it's true – I can transport myself back to that heady mixture of anticipation and wonder in a flash. It wasn't without worry, though: I thought I was going to look like a complete idiot at the workshop and everyone else would know what they were doing! Actually, the truth of the matter is that I didn't even know what to expect. I didn't know the format of the weekend and I still didn't understand what was happening to me – I hadn't planned or decided to become an animal psychic, and it was all happening in a bit of a vacuum. Despite what had occurred with Dan and Maple, there was also a fear as to whether I would even be able to do it again. Perhaps the experiences I'd had were one-offs?

I finally got there and went into the hall where the event was being held. There was a lovely sense of happiness and friendliness, even if it did feel to me that there were hundreds of people who knew what they were doing and me in the middle of it without a clue. The organizer, Sue, got me settled in immediately.

I found a space just before the opening session and sat there, quite nervously, as Sue's husband gave a speech about Amelia. He spoke of how wonderful it was to have her there, what an inspiring presence she was, and how we would all feel that over the next few days. Then Amelia herself came into the room – it was really rather magical, the way she almost floated into the hall. She's a very charismatic and engaging person, with a theatrical quality about her which both drew me in but also made me feel terribly normal and dull. I couldn't help but think: *If that's what animal communicators are like, I don't have a hope.* I could never be like her, I thought – there was such an ethereal quality about how Amelia presented herself, while I sat there in my old jeans and T-shirt, shattered, feeling guilty about leaving my daughter on her birthday weekend, and watched her, tinkling and beautiful, weaving her spell on all of the people gathered.

Amelia began to talk to us about the magical things that I was only just opening up to and the way she spoke made it seem as if it was the most natural thing in the world, as if it was completely normal to talk with animals. I sat there thinking *I don't think it's normal at all* – and it wasn't, at least not for me. I was still coming to terms with it. I'd had the drive down from Scotland to the Lake District to replay what had happened with Dan and Kairyn. To be honest, the initial euphoria about how right I had seemed to be about so many things was starting to wear off a little. In place of it was doubt, as well as a little voice that kept whispering, *What on earth do you think you're doing?* On the trip, I had been wondering whether I had anything at all to compare this to. All I could come up with was the few episodes of 'The Dog Whisperer' that I'd watched on TV and a vague memory of the Dr Dolittle story when I was a girl. I got a little distracted thinking about the guy who is the dog whisperer and realized that I had always really liked how he uses expressions of energy where the dogs pick up on what their human guardians feel. I realized that this sense of energy was exactly what I had got from Dan and Maple. For a moment I dared to dream that maybe I'd be a new version of that – maybe I'd be the pet whisperer . . .

I pulled myself back to the present as Amelia continued with her spiel and talked about her background, which was in dancing. This must be where her presence and theatrics came from, I thought, but what really registered was when she explained how she had found out about her own talent in animal communication, about how it had all seemed bizarre to her at the beginning, and how she had questioned whether this could possibly be happening to her. These words gave me comfort because they resonated with my own experience, and I decided that all I could do for the next few days was 'go with the flow'.

The workshop involved a lot of practical work and I admit that I felt very nervous when I was told that many animals would be brought into the hall at different times. We were told that we could all practise our skills and that we shouldn't expect anything or project our own needs on to the 'guests', but should just take what was there, welcome it, and thank them for anything they chose to give. *Oh my Goodness*, I thought. This was so different to what had happened with Dan. What if I got nothing? What if I froze? What if I was scared or a million other things? I kept trying to bring myself back to what I *did* know, what I had learned from my work with damaged and challenging clients: if there were children or adults who wanted to tell me something, I would be an irresponsible fool not to listen. That would be the line I would take here.

There were a few animals brought in for us to work with – to listen to, to see if we could pick anything up from them, and, I must be honest, I got very general information which I could easily explain away. Looking back on it, I don't think I was giving myself much credit; had I been watching someone else do what I was doing, I'd probably be pretty impressed – but we all tend to be a bit more critical with ourselves, don't we?

At lunchtime I got chatting to a woman who seemed friendly and open. 'I think I'm getting this all wrong,' I confessed to her. 'With that last dog, I got an image of a blond, curly-haired child in red Wellington boots and dungarees, but none of that came up on feedback.' I was delighted when the other woman said that she had got exactly the same image – it was a striking one, and not something a bit non-specific, such as a dog playing with a ball or catching a stick, so we both decided to pluck up courage and talk to the dog's guardian. I wouldn't have been brave enough to do it on my own, but I was happy to be part of a team approach. The woman confirmed that there was a child like that in the dog's world and I was so pleased, not only because I had I picked up on it but also because someone else at the event had seen it too, which had made me more likely to believe the truth of the scene I had been sent.

I went back to the afternoon session of the first day feeling optimistic and positive. I had one 'under my belt' and maybe things would get even better. I was surprised to see not a dog, or cat, or horse, but a guinea-pig this time – I genuinely hadn't thought of working with creatures so small, and a part of me wondered just how interesting such an animal could be. After all, didn't they pretty much spend all their time sleeping on straw or running round little plastic wheels?

Amelia continued her role as facilitator – she would direct and guide us as to what questions we were to ask Daisy the guinea pig, and I found this very useful, bearing in mind that as yet I had no structure regarding how I went about this. Dan had been in charge of our conversations, so it was really helpful to learn that there were foundation stones for any communication. 'How many others does she share her home with?' asked Amelia. An image flashed into my mind, as strong and as clear as a photograph – *four mice live in the run with Daisy*. I wrote my answers down and contributed to the feedback at the end. The young woman who had brought Daisy in looked at Amelia when I said what I had received, almost apologetically. 'No,' she said, 'I'm sorry – there aren't any mice, we don't keep any.' I felt embarrassed and hoped someone else would come in with what they had discovered. As others were making their contributions, a woman behind Daisy caught Amelia's attention and spoke to us all. 'I'm her mum,' she said, pointing to the younger lady who was holding the guinea-pig, 'and I just wanted to say to that woman . . .' at this she waved over to me, clearly not caring that I was beetroot red by this point, 'that she's absolutely right. Two winters ago we looked after some wild mice for friends when they went on holiday – four mice, and they lived in the run with Daisy. She seemed to really enjoy their company and was much livelier when they were around.'

I felt so happy! I had got something that wasn't just right but also wasn't totally obvious. Amelia was really supportive and said that sometimes the person with the animal doesn't always get it straight away or make the right connection immediately. That is something I realize more and more as time goes on – we forget, but animals don't. If an animal continues to send me an image or a word or a feeling, I now know to unpack it over and over again until I know its importance or relevance. I owe it to the animal who is so generously communicating with me, and I have no right to give up on the message simply because it doesn't take two seconds to decipher or the guardian can't make sense of the information immediately.

We were then asked if Daisy had had a litter. Again, in a flash, I felt contractions. I automatically knew what the pain was – by this stage in my life I'd had two children; I knew what contractions felt like and here in the workshop I physically felt them. I didn't say anything at that point, as I didn't want to monopolize things, so when Amelia asked the guardian whether Daisy was a mum I was confused by the reply, which was firmly negative. As shy as I felt about voicing my thoughts and looking like a complete idiot in front of all these people, I needed to comprehend why I was having such an intensely physical response within my own body to the pregnancy question when Daisy had never been pregnant! I couldn't fathom why that would happen. The drive to know and understand what I was experiencing gave me the courage to put up my hand. 'I know you just said that she hasn't had a litter but I've had two children and . . . well, I know what labour pains are like and that's what I felt when I focused in on Daisy. I felt actual physical pushing, real contractions in my stomach when I asked her whether she'd had a litter.'

Amelia just stood there, nodding with her head to the side, very thoughtfully taking it in, then she smiled and said she'd felt it too. She was tuning in to Daisy and checking with her. According to Amelia, it turned out this poor creature had suffered from phantom pregnancies and had thought that she was going to have babies, believed she was going to have babies, wanted to have babies, and it never happened. We were told that was why she loved the mice so much – they had been her surrogate children.

Amelia asked her guardian about some of Daisy's behaviours, which it turned out she displayed all the time, and pointed out that she was nesting, preparing for her babies coming. They never came. She never got them. I was in tears by this stage – to think that I had been so flippant about another creature's experiences when she had suffered so much. I truly believe that was the moment when I realized how similar all of us animals are, human and non-human. The pain Daisy had sent to me was that which only a mother could recognize and I found it terribly emotional that she had never been able to fulfil that most basic need. If I could cross that bridge of communication and reach out to another it would be a privilege, even if it meant I would have to feel pain myself in the process.

I completely believed what Daisy had told me, and what Amelia had confirmed – now, I just had to believe in myself.

Chapter 5

My Past, My Present, My Future

As we all packed up after the session with Daisy, Amelia came over to me and said, 'Well done.' It was only for a second, but I felt so pleased and rather proud, as if the trip had definitely been worthwhile and this was something that I could genuinely make part of my life.

The next day, the group was set the task of doing some meditation work. We were to ask the people who had stopped us or discouraged us from communicating with animals to step forward, then we were encouraged to deal with our unresolved business with them and send them away. I found this quite challenging. Some of those around me had been working with animals for years, and they had been ridiculed or even prevented from making the communication. I was in a completely different position, given that it was only a few days since I had first embarked on this journey of discovering my psychic ability and, as yet, all of my experiences had been positive, even if I had been thrown in at the deep end.

That wasn't to say that I'd had a straightforward life – far from it – it was just that none of it related to animals. When we were all doing the feedback from the session, everyone else was able to identify who they had seen when they were 'clearing out the attic', as it was called, but my attic was stowed out. I had so many people in there I didn't know where to start. When it was my turn to report back to the group, I admitted that my experience was quite different – I had my mum, my dad, my grandmother, my aunts, uncles, lots of people hanging around in my mind, and I didn't know who to focus on. Amelia said that she'd had the same experience initially and that it means that there have been lots of people in your life who have squashed your abilities or talents and they're all there to give you a chance to move things on. That actually made sense to me, but then Amelia very quickly said, 'Your dad's passed over but he's here today with you.' She said it in a flash as if it had just hit her, and she was right: my father had died two years earlier. Her next words threw me. 'He's here to help you because he communicated with animals too and he wants to help,' she said. 'He really wants to be there for you.'

I just looked at her and said, 'That'd be a first.'

She didn't know my background, but the thought of my dad doing anything for me in this life or the next would have been laughable. He and my mum had separated when I was young, and, although he had maintained some sort of contact with us, it was next to useless. He was unreliable, thoughtless, and never even made a financial contribution to the lives of my sister and me. As a result, I had cut him out of my life as a teenager when he had let me down once too often, but, once I'd had my own children, I'd made some sort of peace with him so that Nathan and India would have their grandfather. It was hard. I still harboured resentments, but now that I had completed my therapy training, I understood him in a different way and was able to make my peace with him before he died.

As all of this was racing through my mind, Amelia continued to speak. 'Your dad wasn't around for you much, was he? He didn't give you much when he was here?' I could feel the emotion starting to well up as I replied. I was acutely aware that we were having this very private conversation in front of all these other people. 'No. No, he certainly did not.'

'That's why he's here now,' she told me gently. 'He wants to help you. He was there when you worked with Daisy and he will be there when you do this work. He communicated with animals and found the whole process incredibly painful, so painful that he shut down from it. He wanted to spare you that same pain; that's why he discouraged you and prevented you from being passionate about animals – it was because he wanted to prevent you from going through the same pain that he'd gone through. Take comfort from that.'

Could that be true, I wondered? As a child I was always scared of animals. Other children may have constantly been on the lookout for waifs and strays to take home, but that was never me. If I saw a dog a hundred yards away,

I'd scream and hide behind my mum. I was terrified of them and had absolutely no inclination to be anywhere near them. My sister kept her eyes peeled all the time, hoping there might be a dumped kitten or puppy that she could scoop up and beg to keep, but I'd run a mile rather than be anywhere near what I thought were scary, frightening creatures who only wanted to attack me.

Samantha was two years younger than me and she spent her childhood following her adoration of animals. She couldn't get enough of them and always seemed to find some creature or other that had been abandoned and needed to come live with us. It would drive me bonkers, as I didn't feel drawn to them at all. My mum must have felt the same, as she would just take them to the local rescue centre the next day. Every summer holiday, Samantha would bring the little furries from school and I'd put up with them in the bedroom. Those long weeks didn't go any quicker with the scratching and scuffling of numerous hamsters and guinea-pigs as a backdrop! Now I was contemplating a life with animals at the centre of it every day. My dad, when he was there, had never encouraged me to face my fears – was that because he thought it was better for me to stay away from animals? I tried to take on board what Amelia had told me, and I silently said *thanks* to him.

The rest of the weekend passed quickly. I managed to get a lot of useful, and accurate, information from the animals I communicated with. Amelia closed the event by saying how much she'd enjoyed the time we'd all spent together and that she had one last message to pass on – she said that she saw great things for some of us, and there was definitely someone who would go into the media and write books. I knew who she was talking about – or at least I thought I did. I was sure it would be the woman three seats down from me who had done some brilliant work every single day.

On the way home, I had continuous mental chatter going on with my dad. Following on from what I'd learned, I actually thanked him for all the pain and the trauma in my life as that had taken me to where I was at this point. If I hadn't had that experience, I wouldn't have opened up to what I knew now. A lot of things were coming together and I remembered that he had spent a lot of his retirement watching wildlife programmes on Sky. He had a dog by then and when I'd visited him with the kids I'd automatically presumed it was his new wife who'd wanted one. When I'd asked her, she'd said, 'No, it was your dad, you know how soft he is with animals.' I was very surprised at that time but I also realized that I knew very little about him. Amelia had said that his experience with animals was ridiculed and I could believe that. My dad was raised in the tough Gorbals of Glasgow – showing sensitivity and talking to animals wouldn't have exactly been the done thing.

He'd had a very hard life. What I learned as an adult was that he'd had a very difficult relationship with all his siblings. His mother was German and had come to Britain during the Second World War after meeting my grandfather, a Scottish soldier. She'd fled Germany and had been separated from her family, who didn't manage to escape, leaving her in a foreign country which had recently seen her as the enemy. I know that my granny was treated disgustingly by the people around her: she'd had excrement smeared on her door, was called a Nazi and told to go back to where she came from – in fact, she was despicably received in this country. The amazing thing was that if you'd met her you'd never have known she was German. She worked really hard to hide her accent and actually sounded as Glaswegian as you could get. She had been thrown in at the deep end. My grandfather was not a good husband and at the end of the 1950s she left, with their eight children, to squat in a two-bedroom flat, a life with no support.

Whenever I thought of her I always felt there was an amazing line of courage and strength running through my family. She was a hard woman and as a grandmother she wasn't warm – there was no love shown, there were no cuddles, and she wasn't demonstrative at all. My dad was the eldest of them all and he had been given, without invitation, the role of the father – this was something he just had to accept and it was forced on him by my grandmother's choices, but it was also what made him the man, and the father, he turned out to be. He was an alcoholic, a poor husband and a lousy dad, but the things Amelia said to me at the workshop made more sense than they would have done ten years before. Things were falling into place.

As I drove home, having a conversation with my father, forgiving him and questioning him, I felt as if he was there. At one point it was as if he very clearly told me to get in touch with his second wife and tell her she must go to a spiritualist church so that he could communicate with her. I found all this odd – in some ways, more so than I had with Dan. I guess with animals there was still some distance, but if this really was my dad communicating with me, it changed everything in a different way: would everyone who had once been in my life now be able to tell me things? I also got the sense from my dad that I should embrace what was happening to me, and a real feeling of love and warmth when that message came through – given what my relationship with my dad had been like for so many years, this was nothing short of a miracle.

I was missing the kids by now – and I was also missing my dog, Lady. I wondered whether I could use what I'd learned and actually contact her. She was always very concerned when I was away from home for even a little while, so I had no idea how she would have coped at my sister's while I was gone for days on end. I sent her positive images of me driving up, walking in the door and greeting her.

All of a sudden, as I was trying to communicate with Lady, I heard a voice. I knew it was in my head but it was as clear as if someone was in the car with me. It was shouting, *Slow down! Slow down!* I was on a hairpin bend on a winding back-road in the middle of nowhere. I immediately hit the brake and the speed dropped incredibly quickly as a red car came racing towards me, round the bend, over the hill, creeping over the cat's-eyes into my lane.

If I hadn't dropped my speed so quickly, there was no way we could have avoided each other.

I'd missed a head-on collision by seconds – if that.

I drove on, shaking, absolutely convinced that it was Lady who had been telling me to slow down. She'd saved my life and I could hardly wait to see her.

When I was about two minutes away from my sister's house, I parked so that I could call and say I'd be there very soon. 'Can you observe Lady?' I asked Samantha. 'Just look to see whether she seems to know that I'm on my way.' My sister was a bit confused – she knew nothing at this point about what had been happening to me, and I'd just told her I was going on some sort of training weekend – but she assumed I was just missing my lovely dog and hoped she'd been missing me too.

I drove on to her house and rang the bell full of excitement, desperate to hold the dog I was sure had saved my life. Samantha opened the door.

'Where is she?' I asked, looking around for Lady. 'What did she do?' I imagined a warm, fuzzy scene with my dog and me communicating like never before.

My sister looked at me as if I was mad. 'Well, when you rang the bell, she growled like someone was coming to kill her, and now she's gone looking for food – is that what you were after?'

I smiled at her words – brought down to reality with a bump!

Chapter 6

Listening and Learning

As the days passed and I thought about what had happened in the Lake District, I realized that this whole new world which was opening up to me was one to which I was now very strongly drawn. It intrigued me. I wanted to be part of this amazing new phenomenon. Unlike most people, though, I didn't rush out and buy books or scour the internet for information – I wanted to just 'go with the flow' and build my knowledge through practice. And I now knew that what I really needed was more 'hands-on' experience, more creatures on which I could practise my skills. I contacted as many people as I could think of, locally, every friend I'd ever had, people from the workshop – if I had their number or email address, they heard from me! I told everyone I met. Of course, I was a little cautious in what I said – it wouldn't have been advisable to rush up telling complete strangers that I thought I could talk to animals, asking if they had anyone they'd like me to have a chat with – but I did say that I was trying to develop my communication skills and that I hoped to be able to pick up on emotional messages from other creatures.

One of my first clients was a beautiful tortoiseshell cat called Mitzi, who lived in England. One of the first things I had to deal with was what I would call the people who cared for the animals I would be in touch with – were they 'owners'? This felt like rather a strange, almost insulting term to use. I was already feeling a very close link with animals, despite my years of wariness, and I recognized a discomfort in the suggestion that we, as some sort of 'superior' animal, owned others. I know that some people may think I'm being too soft or over-emotional, but I decided that I would refer to the human carers as the 'mum' or 'dad' of my clients, and those are still the terms I use to this day.

In those early sessions, I also decided something else: in order to avoid putting the information from the mums and dads on to any reading, I didn't ask them what they wanted me to investigate or ask about any character traits until I had first tried to make some contact with the animal. By doing this, I started with a clean sheet and I could feed back to them whatever was given to me. As a result, if I got things right, I would feel more confident – and the person who had asked me to do the reading would also feel more sure about what I was doing, were I able to tell them things I really shouldn't have known. Now that I know my gift isn't a fluke, I no longer feel the need to prove myself every time; to begin with, though, I was confirming things to myself as much as to anyone else.

This first session after the workshop raised an interesting aspect of animal communication work for me. I had been surprised to find that most animal communicators did the vast majority of their readings by distance – that is, they aren't physically present beside the animal they are working with. While I accepted this was indeed possible (after all, it had happened to me with Dan) I didn't imagine that it could work simply by looking at a photograph. However, Amelia had asked us all to bring a photograph of an animal to 'read' at the weekend and it completely blew me away that not only was it possible to connect with the animal from the photograph, but it was easier to work from a photograph than with a live animal!

As my experience of communicating with animals has grown so has my learning and I quickly concluded that working from photographs is incredibly beneficial on many different levels. Firstly, it allows me to work with animals all over the world. Secondly, because travel is not required, urgent cases can be dealt with immediately. Thirdly, and most importantly, I have found that it is often much better for the animal – particularly if it is in pain or stressed, as the presence of a stranger invading their space could be far from comforting and may make communication more difficult. If they are invited to communicate from a distance, in the comfort of their own homes, they may be more open to contact and thus my opportunity to help them is maximised.

However, I wondered whether people would believe

that working from a photograph was possible? I knew the results would speak for themselves and the guardians would be able to see just how well distance communication and healing worked, and so I began my work with Mitzi's photograph.

I started by doing a full body scan on her as we had been taught by Amelia. This is where you ask the animal's permission to energetically enter their physical self so you can work through the body – feeling, seeing or sensing what is wrong. Not all animals are entirely comfortable with this concept, but I've found that with gentle reassurance all animals give permission and most actually enjoy the experience. Nowadays, while I still teach students how to scan the body in that way, I rarely use the process myself, as my energy sensitivity is such that I'm very quickly just 'pulled' to the area that's causing problems, even before I even ask. This can happen when talking with guardians on the phone – and even when reading emails. With Mitzi, however, it was all new to me, so I used the scanning procedure I'd just learned from the workshop.

The entire process has to be done with an open heart and an open mind. All information that comes through has to be accepted, and I realize that not everything will be clear to me immediately and that nothing should be discounted. Perhaps at the start of my journey I didn't realize this as much as I do now. To begin with, I breathe deeply and make a conscious decision to recognize anything that is wrong with my own body. If I know my own aches and pains from the outset, there will be less risk of attributing those to the animal. I then make the psychic connection with the animal, letting it know that I would like to communicate and asking for permission to do so. If the animal gives permission, I then explain what the body scan is and ask if it is OK to proceed. A body scan is where I psychically enter the body of the animal and merge my energy with their energy. This allows me to 'be' them, so I can see through their eyes, hear through their ears, feel their emotions and physical pain. Once I have entered their body through the top of their head (through the crown chakra), I visualize travelling through their body, from the head to the tail, working my way through, focusing on every single part individually and noting down a flash of pain or a sudden ache whenever it happens. Of course, some animals are fine and the body scan is swift – but this wasn't the case with Mitzi. Body scans can take a long time, especially if there are a lot of problems. Every time you pick anything up during a body scan it is vital that you pay acute attention to whatever that is and re-check it before moving on to the next area. At the end, I always visualise myself leaving the animal's body, coming out of it, back into my own and disconnecting from them. This ensures that our energies are no longer merged and neither of us can take on the issues of the other. I then thank them for allowing me to work so intimately with them.

I admit that I was nervous about doing this with Mitzi, because I was on my own, away from the workshop group, and really facing up to the question of whether or not I had any talent in this world at all, but the issues came thick and fast at so many stages of the scan that I simply couldn't deny what I was feeling. Her left front leg was very sore in the thigh area – in fact it felt out of alignment – and her right front leg was also stiff. Her throat was constricted when she meowed and she couldn't swallow smoothly. The poor thing had a stiff spine and a sore stomach, some discomfort in her left eye and some damage to her upper left molars. There was such a lot coming through about so many aches and pains that I wondered whether I was making some of it up. At one point my own ankle became very painful at the front, slightly towards the left, and I felt this very distinctly. After the body scan I got the distinct impression of two other cats, but this was accompanied by a heavy feeling, which I interpreted as sadness, the meaning of which I was unsure of. Before I read the information sent by her mum, I asked Mitzi what she thought might help her and she told me raw fish, but she was also very clear that she needed to be near to or on grass. Her final response to that question was that she needed yellow in her life – I wasn't surprised, as this is the colour of the solar plexus, which supports the stomach and digestive system, an area I felt she was really having trouble with.

Mitzi seemed like a very intelligent cat – I got the phrase

wise old bird – and I wondered whether she had any views about any medication she might be on (I suspected she must be on something, as there seemed to be so many aches and pains related to her). A flash came to me of her 'sicking' tablets up, which I interpreted as Mitzi not wanting to take them because she didn't think they were any good for her, and I felt my own breathing quicken and my stomach push out, almost as if it were swelling. Because she was my first case the pressure was on and I *really* needed and wanted to get it right, so I spent a lot of time with her and got a huge amount of information. As we continued to communicate Mitzi started sending me clearer requests – *I have headaches,* she told me. *Tell my mum and dad that I have headaches.* I promised that I would.

As I continued to look at her photograph I was flooded with the feelings of love she had for her human family, as well as getting an image of a deep-purple cushion. I then looked at the questions her mum had sent me to ask: *Can you please help with our much-loved 20-year-old cat? We'd love to know what she wants and what she needs to make her life more comfortable. She is on medication but is very unhappy taking it – although she doesn't seem to be in pain, she's getting weaker and, given her age, we don't know what to do for the best.* None of this surprised me – Mitzi's advanced age was clearly the main reason for all of her ailments.

Her mum had another request. *Can you please also ask her to stop catching birds?* This immediately drew my attention and raised an ethical issue for me. Should I ask a cat to stop chasing birds? Was it right for me to make that request from one human through another, to ask a cat to stop doing the very thing which came absolutely naturally to it? As the questions went through my mind, a resounding *NO!* also rang in my ears, and I made a decision there and then that I have always stuck to. At that point I decided that if a natural behaviour is doing the animal no harm, and is merely something that a human would prefer to stop, I wouldn't pass on the request. I would never use communication as a tool to control natural behaviour. In fact the issue of birds did come up, as Mitzi sent me images of her catching them as well as waves of happiness when she did so. She also seemed very pleased at the image of a bird table, but I couldn't quite work out why her mum would have one of these: she'd made it clear to me that she didn't like birds at all, which was why she wanted Mitzi to never catch them. I tried to ignore the bird table but the determined cat kept sending the image to me so I simply put it aside for later.

When I went back to her mum with my findings, I was delighted to find that so much of it had been accurate – one of the main things Mitzi had been keen to inform them about was the *poorly stomach*, as she called it, and her mum confirmed that she had severe kidney problems. (In fact she died of kidney failure about four months after my reading.) I had asked Mitzi how she would want to pass – the amount of physical problems she had exhibited had made me sure this would not be far in the future – and she was adamant that she did not want veterinary help; she wanted to be able to go on her own. This was something that I absolutely had to tell her mum. We humans find it one of the hardest things to deal with: advances in science mean that we can keep our beloved pets with us for perhaps longer than nature would decree, but we also have the horrible decision to make regarding whether or not to have them 'put to sleep'. If a pet has been ill, that decision is even stronger in our minds, as suffering is the last thing we want them to endure – and yet how can we be absolutely sure it is what the animal would want? Perhaps they would be willing to bear the pain for longer, perhaps they want to live no matter what – or, indeed, perhaps they've had enough and feel it is time to pass over.

I knew there were things that could be done for Mitzi that would make her time with her human family more comfortable, but I also knew that the end was not far away. When I'd asked her what would make her life happier or better she'd sent me an image of a cat basket piled high with off-white pillows, cushions and blankets; I also saw a picture of the outdoors, with a cat under a tree. I knew that contact with the earth is important to cats and that Mitzi would need to be taken there if she was unable to walk. When I checked with her mum about the sleeping area 'piled high' with off-white bedding, she confirmed that Mitzi liked to sleep on her and her husband's bed, which had ivory covers, as well having a creamy, furry blanket of her own which was also on the bed. I now know that a cat or dog will often send me an image of a pet basket to symbolize a sleeping area even if that isn't exactly where they sleep – they are using shorthand to help the poor, slow-witted human communicator! I really hoped that her mum and dad would take her out to the grass, no matter how weak she was, and I also made a note to myself to check in with them in a few months' time to see how Mitzi was doing.

Although Mitzi's story was a sad one, for me she had been very much loved and had lived to a ripe old age. She adored her mum and dad, and there was devotion between all parties involved. I had to tell myself that a cat living in happiness until she was twenty was not something I could get too upset about: I would no doubt have much sadder stories to deal with.

Some of the things I did with Mitzi I no longer practise. To begin with I would ask questions such as *What is the colour of your food bowl? Where do you sleep?* I don't ask these questions now because, while I often get accurate replies, it's not usually important to the animal – they just want to get on to the nitty-gritty of what's bothering them. Similarly I learned that I sometimes needed to leave aside aspects of a message that doesn't seem to make sense and come back to it later. Often it is when I make time to think specifically about a message that it becomes clear. In Mitzi's case I realized that the bird table that got Mitzi so excited was actually something that she *wanted* rather than something that was actually in her world. An old cat who loved chasing birds but who knew her mum was scared of them could think of nothing better than a table set up in her garden providing easy pickings all day long. It was nothing more than a beautiful fantasy for Mitzi.

Over the next few weeks I did more and more animal communication sessions, and the feedback was all reassuring me, bit by bit, that I could actually do this.

I did get a fright with one client, however. I had been asked to work with a horse called Storm and, as soon as I tuned into him, all I received was the word 'evil'. It took me a little while to get past that because all I felt was, indeed, a presence of evil. I actually felt scared. It made it so difficult to tune into him, as I couldn't get past that presence, and I also thought that I clearly wasn't 'doing it right', which made me feel awful. How could I possibly be thinking that a horse was evil when I had been taught that animals simply aren't like that? How could I possibly be getting it so wrong, and what on earth would I tell Storm's mum?

When I gave her the feedback, I tried to be sensitive and said that her horse could be a bit 'bad-tempered'. She laughed immediately and said, 'Absolutely! Not many people can work with him – in fact, not many people want to.' I felt a little braver after that response and said that the word 'evil' had come into the session. She laughed again. 'Oh yes – plenty of people have called Storm evil in his time. He doesn't keep his feelings hidden if he doesn't like someone.' What a relief – I had got it right. The lesson I learned from Storm was to trust what I got and to recognize that animals have moods too, just like us.

I was, by now, getting a reputation for the quality of the communications I was getting from animals, and the work was coming in thick and fast. What was becoming obvious to me was that my strongest talent was in the area of claircognisance. This is a type of perception that isn't related to seeing or hearing something, it isn't a smell or a taste, and it isn't something that can be pinned down easily. It is simply the way in which I *just know* something without knowing how I know it. It's something which anyone reading this book has probably experienced with their own animals but, for me, it is heightened. If you have a cat, I bet you *just know* when it's off colour, even though it can't possibly look paler or flushed. Dog guardians frequently *just know* when their animal is a bit down or out of sorts and it has nothing to do with their appetite or running a temperature. We all, very often, *just know* when animals we love are unwell or sad or lonely long before physical symptoms kick in, and this is because we are so attuned to them. For me, that attunement comes with every creature I work with, and they can transmit their facts to me in a form of 'energy shorthand' that reaches my consciousness immediately, with no prior thought. This is what makes my life as a pet whisperer so difficult to explain to people who are closed to the whole idea of animal communication – think back to the last time you *just knew* that your sister was going to phone, long before the telephone rang. What about that time you *just knew* there would be an accident in the family before anyone had even left the house? Recall episodes when you asked someone how they were and they chirped back 'great!' and you didn't believe them? You *'just knew'*, didn't you?

Now multiply that feeling by a thousand – and apply it to animals. Is it any wonder I'm just a bit cautious when telling people what I do?

Chapter 7

Meeting Dan

It is very hard not always knowing the endings to stories, but over the years I have had to learn my own boundaries. It's a privilege to be allowed these glimpses into other lives, but sometimes I do have to move on. With Mitzi the cat, I found this difficult. I knew from the sessions I'd had with her that she didn't have much time before she passed. However, I also knew that her major concern – of being allowed to cross the rainbow bridge of her own accord at a time of her own choosing – was of the utmost importance to her, and I personally needed to know whether that had happened at the end. I contacted her mum, who told me: 'Poor Mitzi got weaker and weaker. It was a very painful time but we felt less stressed than we would have done otherwise – we would have constantly been asking ourselves if we should call the vet to come to the house. Knowing she wanted to pass by herself and not be helped by the vet, we spent those last days and hours cuddling her. Although very weak, she had moved herself further up the bed until her head was on my pillow and she took her final breath.'

Mitzi had told me that she had been with her mum pre-viously in the form of a small brown dog – I didn't know if this was a small breed of dog or a puppy – and that the number 8 was significant. I had passed this information on, but it was only later that I was told her mum had had a beagle . . . when she was eight years old! This gave me the hope that Mitzi, if she wanted to, would find a way of coming back and being with those who had loved her so much again, but I didn't feel that it was an appropri-ate time to raise this. There is such grief when an animal passes over, no matter how much their human family has done for them, and sometimes the thought of that animal returning in another form isn't necessarily comforting, as it can feel almost a betrayal to not continue grieving.

I had also been continuing to work with Dan during this time, primarily sending him some fairly intensive healing to deal with his sadness and sense of loss over the little boy he'd loved, but also to calm him as he did still have anger issues that Kairyn worried would result in him being aggressive and perhaps even biting some-one. I found it amazing that he had that side to him – Dan was such a lovely dog when we communicated. He had been my first real communication, having kick-started all of this for me, and I had such a pull to him. As we did more and more work together I felt how much better he was, and that his anger was decreasing.

Kairyn had by now given me a photograph of him and this really helped. As stated earlier, I now prefer to work with photographs rather than on a one-to-one basis, because this allows me to work without being distracted by the animal or their behaviours as well as allowing the animal to communicate without worrying about meeting a new person in the flesh, perhaps being in a different environment, with confusing smells, and all sorts of things that can make the process less effective for all parties. I was informed at the workshop that digital photographs were less successful for connecting with animals, but luckily I've never found that to be the case.

I still wanted to work with Dan even though I had quite a lot of cases: he mattered to me. So when Kairyn initially gave me his photograph at dog training, I was delighted. He was so beautiful and majestic in the image, lying on a bed like a king. I had actually put into one of my feedback reports that he was royal, and this was confirmed by what I saw – there was a real sense of him owning the space. I said so to Kairyn and she replied that the picture made her think he was telling his minions to peel him another grape. We laughed. I felt like I knew him.

I had done five sessions with Dan, focusing on giving him healing therapy. He still had lots of emotional stuff hanging around, but the anger and grief were dissipating. He was opening up more and that was also being recognized at home, where he was less defensive, but he still had issues. While he was more affectionate and less guarded, Dan's behaviour still had a long way to go. I was so excited when, one evening after class, Kairyn asked if

I'd like to meet him. I jumped at the chance. I was completely in love with this animal. Every time I tuned in the energy was so good and it felt so loving. He always bounced up to meet me, psychically, as if he couldn't wait. I felt his eagerness and was really excited about meeting him.

We agreed that Kairyn would bring him to my house and I spent the morning as excited as a teenager bringing her boyfriend back home for the first time. Kairyn had warned me not to fuss over him, as he hated that, but I desperately wanted to. I owed this dog so much: he'd truly opened my eyes to what I was capable of, and I would have been happy to cuddle him and fawn over him all day long.

It had been such a long wait, but I did as I was told and stood there. I put my hand out and waited for him to come over before I started stroking his fur. Despite my excitement and all our communication I was a bit anxious, because I knew he was still prone to aggression, but I didn't feel scared, at least not overly so, so I continued petting him. Then all of a sudden Kairyn snapped, 'Get back!' I did this as quickly as I could, and she told me that she was worried Dan might go for me.

After all we'd been through and shared, after all the work I'd done with him and for him, and with all the romantic notions I'd had in my head, the last thing I thought would happen would be that Dan would want to attack me. It was quite a lesson. I realized that you can't make assumptions about what's acceptable to an animal just because you've got a lovely connection with them and you've been doing lots of good work, where you're both feeling it and everybody's seeing it. That was a real message for me: never think that it's all right to invade an animal's space without permission.

Kairyn put Dan back in the boot of the car and I did all other work with him from a distance. It felt like love when I did the sessions – in fact, the whole reason for this book is that I didn't have that connection with animals until Dan came along. Pretty much every time I tuned in, it was like he was eagerly waiting for me, really happy to see me, and I could feel all this positive, loving energy. Although he did have occasional moments when he was angry and frustrated, more often there was a feeling of absolute love and it was beautiful. That was why I felt the way I did when we met – whereas for Dan, that day, it wasn't like that at all. I checked in with him later and all he would say was, *Don't assume that just because I let you communicate with me you can take liberties.* Distance communication was started on Dan's terms and that was how he wanted it to continue. I would never take any animal for granted or assume I have a right to expect certain behaviour from them simply because there has, at one point, been a loving psychic link.

Some people ask what this psychic link actually is, what animal communication actually is. I'm not sure how to define something which now seems so natural to me, but I'll try. I think there is a lot of criticism and cynicism about anything 'psychic', which is why I prefer the term 'animal communication'. To be honest, there are probably plenty of people out there who think I'm absolutely nutty for saying that I can do what I know I can, and the words used to describe what goes on between me and my feathered or furry friends aren't going to make them suddenly decide otherwise. If people don't believe it, fine; but they're missing out on so much. Why would anyone want to cut off part of life, ignore part of our world? You can call me a psychic or animal communicator or pet whisperer or raving lunatic – but I know what I've experienced and I truly believe that anyone reading this book can learn to do the same. *Everyone* has the ability to communicate with animals – they just need to learn how to reignite their innate abilities.

Humans have so many skills that have been lost, or that we simply don't practise or need any more, and it's my belief that, at some time in our history, a contract was made between us and animals in which they agreed to protect us and be our loyal companions in return for our love and care and food. Simply put, the domestic dog evolved out of wolves hanging around tribes of people and eating their meaty leftovers; we then brought them into our lives and the rest is history. It makes my blood boil when I hear of animal cruelty, because I truly feel that it means we haven't kept to our side of the bargain. We have no right to practise selfishness or decree we are better than other animals. We're just different, not superior.

The animals with whom we share our lives and the planet know so much about so many things – and they know an awful lot about us. They pick up on our feelings – hasn't your dog ever sat beside you faithfully while you think of things that hurt you, almost as if he's waiting for you to let the tears flow and sending you a message that he'll be there till they stop? They reflect back to us what we may be trying to keep quiet about – hasn't your cat steadfastly refused to be petted by someone you really don't like, despite the fact that she'll roll on her back for anyone else? Our animals are so in tune with us and our families, and we often let them hear and see things that we would keep from other humans. They listen to phone conversations, watch as we rant about what happened at work that day, see how much we enjoy getting ready to go out with someone we have a secret attraction for – be careful, for they pick up on everything.

They have needs and preferences of their own, but they also remember that contract and look out for us so well. Sometimes our animals do not want to answer our questions, but want to utilize the time to present their messages. I worked with a dog called Hetty whose messages and priorities were very clear indeed. She loved her mum and wanted to thank her for all that she gave, but she was running about and jumping up and down so excitedly from the outset that it was as almost as if she wanted to get the soppy stuff out of the way as quickly as possible.

Her body scan was done very swiftly as there were no physical concerns, and I moved on to her emotional state. Her mum had said she was highly strung for no apparent reason and seemed quite nervous at times; I wanted to find out what would settle Hetty. As soon as I asked her whether there was anything she wanted to communicate to me, she was right in there: *My mum's a right one! Doesn't always know what she wants – and it's usually right under her nose.* I pulled it back to Hetty: *What about you? What do you want?* She was bouncing about all over the place by this time. *I want Mum to laugh more*, she said. *I want her to have more contact with people. I want her to get a man!* I had to laugh at this – was I now running a dating agency? This one would certainly raise some ethical issues; Hetty's mum had asked me to find out why her dog was so animated all the time, and I was going to have to tell her to get her love life sorted before the canine Cupid would settle down. This type of confiding information comes out frequently, but Hetty was so direct with it that I was faced with a dilemma. Still, I had to stick with my own rules and check that I'd got things right, even though it seemed as if there was little room for doubt.

Is that the message for your mum, Hetty? I asked. *Yes! Yes! She's to get a man – and I know the one she needs. Tell her to stop ignoring him and putting him off; tell her she needs to say that she'll go somewhere with him.* Well! I wasn't quite sure how dogs made sense of our dating rituals, and suspected that Hetty thought her mum and this unidentified suitor would be going out for some nice walkies together, but she certainly seemed positive. She was bouncing around, trying to tell me more. *She's hiding behind us*, she told me. I asked her what she meant. *She doesn't get close to people because she is so busy with all her dogs. She uses us as an excuse but we don't want her to be alone – we want her to have a partner too! Tell her to put some make-up on, tell her to dress nicely . . . tell her to let someone look after her the way she looks after us.*

Goodness.

Hetty had nothing else to say to me: Sandra, her mum, was all she was concerned about. After repeated questioning I felt sure that, as soon as Sandra sorted out her personal life, the dog would settle down. Fortunately Sandra was a very warm and approachable woman and I did find enough courage to tell her exactly what had been passed to me – I had no choice; there was no other message. It's my role to advocate on behalf of the animal regardless of the issue. She was actually very emotional about it, though (thankfully) she smiled throughout the feedback. 'It's true,' she said, 'I do hide behind my pets. They're easier to love and they won't hurt me.' There was obviously a lot of history there, but I just needed to make sure Sandra looked to the future Hetty wanted for her.

Sandra never came back for another session – I hope because she took her bouncy dog's advice and found a human companion too. Animals see so much more than we realize, things that perhaps we don't even allow ourselves to see, and they are so lacking in the guile with which we often surround ourselves that their messages always come from a good place. I absolutely love the idea of doggy matchmakers for all of us!

Chapter 8

Dolly's Despair

What I love is when a client is a real chatterbox – and that's certainly what I got with Dolly the chocolate Labrador. It makes my job so much easier when the communication just flows, and she was a really happy, chatty character. All I knew from her mum, Wendy, was that she had had a sad start in life and had now passed over. Wendy wanted to check in with her to see if she was happy on the other side. Dolly's enthusiasm was so overwhelming that I knew immediately that she was delighted with the life she had experienced with her human mum, and I found it quite hard to believe that she had had any sadness in her world at all. However, by this stage, I was also aware that animals can be just as adept as humans at hiding their history, so I was prepared to dig a little deeper.

With some animals, I find that their physical characteristics can actually be felt as I do the reading – it's almost as if their character comes through in the way they move. I learned that Dolly wasn't just a real tail-wagger, like most dogs, but that she had a tendency to move her whole back end when she was communicating. Bizarrely, this happens with me when I am in tune with some animals, and, as I chatted with Dolly, I could feel myself wiggle about in the bottom area, with a rolling sort of movement from side to side! She also made another strange action, which I certainly couldn't copy – I don't have enough legs to do so! Her whole body moved when she wagged her tail in great excitement, but when it really ramped up a notch she lifted herself off the ground entirely. When I checked back in with Wendy at the end of the reading she confirmed that, when Dolly was with her and particularly happy, she'd jump off the ground with all four feet and everyone used to laugh that she would fly with happiness one day.

This was all lovely, but there was another side to Dolly. Wendy confirmed all of the happiness that I got from her, and that her favourite toy had been a ratty old tennis ball, but there was a heartbreaking side to Dolly's story that I had to check with Wendy. I felt that, before Wendy, Dolly had been taken to begin her life somewhere away from her family when she was very young. While the same happens to most puppies, for Dolly it signalled a time of darkness and pain, which came across both in her emotions and in the agonies I got from her body scan.

There were things that had happened to her during that period of her life which caused her physical difficulties forever; even though she had now passed over she still felt it was important to send that information on to me. Her body felt old, yet she felt young at heart. There was so much sadness in her past, but she wanted me to thank Wendy for the love and new lease of life that was given to her and that had allowed her to end her days so much better than the way in which she had started them.

She told me that trust was a huge issue for her, but that she had bonded with her new family almost immediately despite feeling cautious about giving her trust so quickly. Dolly was trying to distract me a little by focusing on the love and thanks she wanted to pass on to Wendy, but that was fine by me. She was avoiding going too deep into what had happened to her as a puppy and before she went to Wendy's home, but I had seen that before in rescue animals and those who had been mistreated. I knew it would be a story of pain, heartache, loss and abandonment – her past had lacked love, affection and warmth and she would share the fulness of her story in her own time.

She felt like a heavy dog and I was continually drawn to her insides, especially her stomach, where there was something very wrong. The best description I could give of what had happened to that area was that it had been 'traumatized'. I also felt that her weight had never helped, but I was getting confusing signals about that. Dolly loved Wendy so much and kept returning to that love. She sent me the most beautiful images of her head in her mum's lap and being snuggled in close – *Tell Mum I love her so much, and I'll always love her for what she did for me*. As she communicated all of this I found myself crying. I always feel animals' pain and sadness deeply but rarely cry actual tears, as I've learned to feel it and let it go. However, before I knew it tears were rolling down my face, my shoulders were heaving, I felt like my heart was breaking and I was making a wailing sort of noise. It was so intense that my fiancé actually came into my treatment room to see if I was all right.

I knew I had to go back to Dolly's misery and work out what had been wrong, because she clearly wanted to share all of this with me. After a little longer, I realized it was definitely all around her stomach. I felt aches in my own tummy, especially around my womb, and sadly I also felt that this poor creature, who had been through so much and who had finally found love, had died of a malignant tumour. As always, I closed off by sending lots of love and healing.

When I reported back to Wendy, the tale of wretchedness she told me was even worse than I had imagined. It turned out that Dolly was quite young when she died – only seven years old – but from an early age she had been used as a breeding bitch at a puppy farm. She had been forced into having a litter every season and was absolutely wrecked by it. She had massive grief issues with her lost puppies and about how she'd been treated. She'd had no emotional contact before her current mum, and was there only to churn out puppy after puppy. Dolly had never really been overweight, but, as a result of her body being stretched so many times by the pregnancies, she did have lots of saggy skin. Although the tumour that resulted in her death had been in her chest, not her stomach, she was a brood bitch and as such it's very likely that she had Caesareans, which explained why the pains I had experienced were all to do with the reproductive area.

Dolly had died as a result of the surgery to remove the tumour, which was something Wendy felt very guilty about. She had had a massive blood clot, despite making a good initial recovery, and Wendy felt awful that she hadn't been there in her last moments as she had always wanted to do with all of her animals. As Wendy told me, 'I have always wanted the last moments for my pets to be with me telling them I love them, and how special they are, and asking them to watch over me until we meet again. I didn't get that opportunity with Dolly and I just need her to know that I loved her so much.' I was able to tell Wendy that her dog knew this beyond a shadow of a doubt, and this comforted her hugely. Dolly had closed the session by saying: *My mum is an angel – and God loves her*. This was absolutely beautiful and said with such pride, like a mother about her child, but with the words came a strong sensation that Wendy was not religious – which was confirmed, though Wendy did say that she believed in fate and in things happening for a reason.

Wendy had been looking into rescuing another 'breeding bitch', but this wasn't going too well as the rescue centre had found another potential family who it seemed would be the ones to get her once her litter had been weaned. The idea had, however, made Wendy wonder what Dolly would make of it all and I felt that this should be my next area of investigation. Very quickly, Dolly sent me a very clear image of another dog, just like her, and the words, *Mum! That's Mum!* This was a little confusing, as the dog looked very like Dolly, but I didn't feel it was her and I didn't know what she wanted me to tell Wendy about this image. I had to unpack it, and keep looking at what the possible meanings were, until I figured out that she was actually showing me her doggy mum, rather than her human one. It turned out that Wendy had previously rescued an older dog, Poppy, who was indeed Dolly's mother, from a lifetime of puppy farming and breeding. She had only found Dolly because she'd initially found Poppy, and now wished to take on another dog from the same circumstances but wanted to know what Dolly thought of it. 'Dolly helped me heal after losing Poppy and for that I will be forever grateful. I know I was so very lucky to have Dolly in my life, especially as a part of Poppy continued with me after she was gone. There were times when I was sure that, if she could, Dolly would have crawled under my skin and been part of me. I know she loved me as much as I loved her and she was the shadow by my side. Dolly seemed content just to be with me, like nothing else on earth mattered . . . It's a beautiful thing to feel and a wonderful gift to be given.' The question remained whether Dolly would feel betrayed by another dog taking her place.

When I went into the next session with Dolly, she couldn't wait to communicate. I got more from her in ten minutes than I get in an hour with most clients.

Immediately she told me: *Tell Mum to have Poppy! Tell her that's good! Tell her that Poppy should be there!* I had to pull her back, and remind her that we weren't talking about her doggy mum, but about a possible new addition to Wendy's world, Katie. *No – Poppy! Tell her to have Poppy!* she insisted. I kept restating that I needed to know how she felt about Katie, but all I got was a feeling of happiness as she said, *Yes, tell Mum to take her – Poppy needs Mum too; they need each other.*

I had to think about this one – and it did eventually fall into place. It took a lot of thought and quite a leap of faith, but eventually the best way I could process it was like this: some animals who have passed over can see things so much more clearly than us, and one of the things they recognize is when the spirit of a lost companion has been reborn in another body. I sometimes imagine these wise, evolved beings sitting on the next level, from a wonderful vantage point, looking at the make-up of everyone in our world and shaking their heads in disbelief at how blind we can be to what is staring us in the face. How often have you got a new kitten or puppy that reminds you exactly of one you've had previously? How often have you been drawn to one in a litter who you feel just strikes at something in you, rings a little bell of recognition? How often has a dog or a cat just decided that you're the one for them, and approached you with such sure emotions and love that you feel you've known each other forever? I had to accept that maybe it's because this is the case – maybe there is something after this life – and it makes sense that animals are much more aware of it than we are.

I now believe that the spirit of an animal who has passed over often comes back to their cherished owner– and if we could recognize that and open up to it, it would make the pain of loss slightly easier to bear. Dolly was telling me something so obvious: Katie *was* Poppy! With this understanding, I knew she couldn't possibly be upset about the new dog coming into her human mum's life. In fact, it was exactly what she wanted – now the two creatures she loved more than anything would be together again. As soon as I cracked it, Dolly was straight back in: *Tell Mum to look out for Poppy's head! Look at what she does with her head!* I gave up – nothing was going to make Dolly call this new dog 'Katie'.

I needed to make clearer sense of it all and needed Wendy's help to do so, so I had prepared a list of questions I wanted to ask her that would help me ascertain whether Poppy had indeed come back. The questions included: 'Why were you drawn to Katie?' 'What was there about her that made you feel she was the dog for you?' 'What were her mannerisms, her idiosyncrasies?' As Dolly had already advised me of certain things for Wendy to look for, I knew that Wendy's answers would ease the introduction of such a controversial subject as the 'afterlife'. But even as I spoke I was still finding all this a bit concerning, as I knew that there was no guarantee that Wendy would get this dog – in fact, from what she had told me, the rescue centre had offered her to another home – but before I could even ask my pre-planned questions, Wendy burst out excitedly: 'Sarah-Jane, I have such good news: I'm getting Katie. The other home has pulled out, and I can have her!' I shouldn't have been surprised – there are so many things in the world of spirit communication that none of us has any control over, and I firmly believe that, if an animal is destined to be with you, the opportunities to bring that about will arise and present themselves – often in the most unusual ways. Now, some will say that if this is the case why can't they just magic themselves out of the horror of puppy farming? I can understand such cynicism, but the concrete barriers and cruelty that humans put in place cannot always be overcome by love and spirituality alone. It would be lovely if animals could just take themselves out of bad situations, but that truly *would* be magical. As things stand, all I can do is try to pass on the messages from the ones with whom I do have the privilege of communicating.

'Katie reminds me so much of Poppy,' Wendy went on. 'She's scared of the world, timid and wary of new people, just how Poppy was when I first met her. I can remember sitting on the floor and waiting patiently until some three hours later, Poppy felt safe enough to approach me. She had been the scared little girl cowering at the back when all the other dogs had come forward to say "Hello". At the same time, Katie reminds me of Dolly in her looks – small but chunky, almost miniature in size but with a big heart wanting to give love and be loved. With Katie, it was like meeting Poppy all over again. I didn't approach Katie; I waited for her to feel comfortable enough to approach me. I knew that she would probably run away after the initial sniff, but I talked quietly to her, trying not to be in any way threatening and to give her time to trust me, just as I'd done with Poppy. I hadn't expected to feel such a pull towards her as I did when I met her, it was overwhelming.'

This all made a lot of sense to me. I feel blessed to hear these messages and to pass them on. Dolly would always adore and be grateful to Wendy. She gave me such beautiful, soulful messages of sheer love – and she loved the idea of her mum saving another girl from repeated mating and litters of pups, just as she had gone through. Dolly was a happy soul and she is still laughing, over on the other side of the rainbow bridge. She had no regrets, no judgements, only love – and lots of it. Her time here on earth was done and she was ready to go. Wendy did see so much of Poppy in her new dog, and that gave her comfort and the ability to keep loving.

We can never fully get over the passing of animals who have shared our lives, for we give parts of our hearts to them – but in opening our minds to the possibility that death is not an end, but is simply another change, we can all hopefully take comfort from what is so very often waiting for us in a new bundle of fluff and love and mischief.

Chapter 9

Life Lessons

The way in which animals feel emotions quickly became one of the first lessons I learned. It is hard to believe that, not so long ago in our history, people thought that animals simply didn't feel – that they had no pain, no grief, no love flooding through their bodies. They were supposedly different to us, lesser, and nowhere near as important.

Civilization has, thankfully, moved on from that way of thinking, but there are still those who consider the emotional experiences of animals to be on a less important plane to those of humans. Judging by what I have witnessed in my communications, I can categorically state that this could not be further from the truth. Recently I, like many others, was extremely touched by the images shown in *National Geographic* of chimps mourning the loss of one of their own. As keepers carried the body of an elderly female chimp from the compound at a reserve, those who remained lined up to pay tribute, standing and witnessing her last journey with mournful eyes. One chimp even had his hand on the shoulder of another, in a common gesture used by humans to console each other.

The way in which these beautiful creatures, so close to us in their genetic make-up, acted and cared for a group member who had passed was one of the strongest visual displays I have ever seen to emphasize just how close we all are.

Many of the animals I have worked with have had traumatic histories, and this is usually because they have been rescued, latterly brought into new, loving homes but still having to deal with the awfulness of their past. The very fact that their new mum or dad has come to me to try to understand the animal's behaviour is testament to their care and affection, but there is only so much any human can do with partial information about an animal's previous life. By communicating with them, I can provide the rest of the pieces necessary to build up the full picture. Sometimes, of course, an animal may not want to go back and revisit the scene of its trauma, and that is entirely their choice; but, equally, there are occasions when animals desperately want to tell someone what has happened and to find a way to work through it.

I learned a lot about the emotional life of animals through my work with Ozzy, a handsome cross Labrador and German shepherd rescue dog who often showed aggression towards unknown people and dogs, sometimes lunging out at them when walking – even when they were on the opposite side of the street. While clearly guarding and protecting his space outside, he was loving and affectionate with his human family and friends.

His guardians were in no doubt that his aggression was rooted in fear and wanted to understand him better in order to support positive change. His mum, Lea, was very concerned about his exhibitions of fear and aggression. She had already tried various methods to overcome the problem, but had seen very little improvement in his behaviour. In fact, it was so bad that he had to be muzzled and couldn't be let off the lead where there were likely to be other dogs around, because there was no way their safety could be guaranteed. He was completely unpredictable, which made walking him very stressful and not the enjoyable experience it should have been.

I did the communication work with Ozzy through photographs and in fact wouldn't have had it any other way. It was partly for my own safety – my experience with Dan had shown me that a dog who seemed fine in an image could have the potential to act completely differently 'in person', so to speak – but also for Ozzy's sake. I was quite sure that he would be unnecessarily stressed by meeting with me in unfamiliar surroundings and I didn't want to put this poor creature through any more. I knew that he was a rescue dog, and I knew the extent of his aggression, but that was it.

Ozzy was actually incredibly friendly when I made contact with him. He quickly told me lots of in-depth information about his past, his current home and his favourite walks. I got the feeling he was trying to make a good impression on me, knowing I was aware of his behavioural problems and wanting to make sure that I realized he was a good dog. I listened patiently, not really needing any of this background but recognizing that it was vital to let Ozzy set the agenda and gain comfort from directing the conversation.

In the middle of telling me about the walks he enjoyed, Ozzy suddenly altered tack: *I want to change*, he told me. *I really want to change.* I knew as much. I wasn't getting bad vibes from this dog, just fear – fear about his own behaviour as much as anything. *Would you like me to help?* I asked. Now, this may seem a ridiculous thing to say, but I believe it's vital to seek the animal's permission at all stages, to ensure he or she has a say in things that will impact on them and their day-to-day lives. This dog didn't know me, and perhaps he only wanted me to pass the message on without being overly involved. I needn't have worried. *Yes! Yes, please!* he quickly answered. *I'd like you and my mum to help – can you do that?* I reassured him that, with his help and application, we could. It was important to make positive changes and also to make Ozzy feel more confident in difficult situations. However, to get there, I had to ask him something that I knew he may react against.

Ozzy? I need you to trust me – I know life has been difficult for you and if you felt able to share it with me it would help me understand how we can best help you. Do you feel able to tell me about your life before you lived with your mum? I felt him tense up. I didn't push, I just waited for him to come back to me.

Do I have to? he asked. *No,* I assured him, *you don't have to do anything you don't want to – but you've told me that you want to be a good dog, that you want to change how you are when you are out on walks, and I really think that in order to do that we have to take away the power of whatever has happened to you in the past.* I knew that he was considering what I'd said and I was delighted when he agreed to try it. There was trepidation coming from Ozzy in waves, but he was a brave dog. In fact, once we delved into what had happened to him, I was in awe of just how deep that bravery was.

I am still amazed at how this gift works and at the information I am blessed to receive, but when animals reveal awful things to me there's no denying that it can be hard. The communication work with Ozzy identified that he had been thrown out of a moving car as a tiny puppy, dumped by callous people who had no idea of the sanctity of an animal's life and did not care about the damage they were doing. As Ozzy passed this information on to me I could feel him shake, but I could also sense the anger in him. He was unable to verbalize much of what had happened, choosing instead to send me heartbreaking pictures of himself, little more than a scrap of life, being thrown to his expected death. That he survived at all showed just how determined he was, but his struggle continued. He had been in a number of homes, but almost always returned to the local re-homing centre because of his aggression. What he also told me – and no one else knew this – was that he had spent a period of his life as a stray. This period of living rough had been when he was thrown out of one home and before he was taken to a rescue centre again, and it was during this time that his hostility and anger had kept him alive. His time as a stray was such a difficult one but his aggression helped him survive – no wonder it was such a hard habit to break.

This survival tool did not leave him when he was rehomed and he quite literally didn't know how else to behave. I found Ozzy not to be an aggressive dog in his communication with me, but a terribly insecure, scared creature who wanted to change so badly because the situation was making him depressed – he just didn't know how to do it. He loved Lea so much and desperately wanted to stay with her and her partner, which was why he was now so glad that someone was communicating with him. He saw it as his sole chance of altering his behaviour and staying in one place for the rest of his life.

It was a moving session and I reported my findings back to Lea. She loved Ozzy a great deal and was happy to work on behavioural therapy as well as allowing me to continue to deal with his emotional trauma. The whole topic of therapy is one which will perhaps seem rather odd to people who may be under the misapprehension that the client actually has to be physically present with the therapist while work is being undertaken. However, because I am already connected psychically with a client during communication work, I can send healing in the same way I sent psychic messages. It's using exactly the same connection, just with a different intention and outcome. By working this way, I'm not restricted by geographical barriers, and the vitally important point of putting the animal at ease is addressed. I really cannot overstress how awful (and unneccessary) it is for an emotionally or physically pained creature to also have to deal with a stranger invading their space.

The rescue centre from where Lea had got Ozzy had confirmed that there was a period of his life they could not account for, which tallied with what he had told me about his life on the streets. The course of therapy work did indeed allow him to release his emotional damage and work on increasing his confidence to enable him to make the changes that he needed to make. Lea reported that he became calmer and more co-operative in what would have previously been tricky situations.

It was some time later that Lea got back in touch, to ask me to do a reading with her mum's new dog as a Christmas present. She updated me on Ozzy, which was great, as I love to hear how animals are doing after my work with them. Not only had Ozzy's behaviour improved so much that he no longer had to be muzzled when out, but also Lea had changed jobs to become a dog walker and – wait for it – Ozzy went out with her and the other dogs, tail wagging and with a big doggy smile all over his face. What a happy result for all – these stories are the ones that make it all worthwhile.

Not all of the emotional difficulties I've encountered are as heartrending as that of a tiny puppy being thrown from a moving car, or that same poor dog being forced to live on the streets, starving and terrified, a victim of human cruelty. Sometimes the emotions are lighter, and these too show the range of feeling all animals have. One beautiful Persian cat called Sophie made me laugh when we communicated. Her mum had asked me to work with her to relieve the stress that was about to happen when the human family went on holiday. They had never put Sophie in a cattery before, having always left her with friends, but this year they had no choice because the friends were going away at the same time. Sophie's mum was very apprehensive about her darling cat being in strange surroundings and wanted me to prepare and reassure her pet. When doing this, I always use the same technique that I began using when I worked with Maple the horse – telling the animal how many 'dark nights' it will be until their mum returns.

Sophie was a little standoffish, as is often the case with pedigrees (and cats in general!), but she was open to communication, probably because she liked lots of information. I spent a lot of time talking her through what would happen, and suggesting ways for her to deal with any concerns she may have, before I was interrupted by a noise that sounded very much like, *Hurrumph!* I asked Sophie if there was something she wanted to tell me, and she did it again. *Hurrumph!* It was rather like a snort, certainly a sound of derision rather than fear. *I will be delighted, absolutely delighted, when they go on holiday*, she told me. That was unexpected. Did she not like her mum? Was there something about her home life that she needed to get away from?

Sophie paused, before graciously allowing me access to her thoughts – *It's just sooooo boring*, she informed me. *So dull to have the same environment, the same experiences day after day – they don't let me out, you know, because I'm so beautiful. They're quite right, of course, but I do get bored. I think it might be rather fun to have an adventure, don't you?* Well! There was nothing to worry about in terms of Sophie's holiday. I tried to be diplomatic about how I phrased my feedback to her mum, and said that she needed more stimulation. Sophie may not have been too concerned about her mum's feelings but I always try to be sensitive with feedback – for both the guardian *and* the animal, because so many animals do worry about us and especially about the prospect of upsetting us. Sometimes humans will bring their pets to me with one problem but it's actually a different aspect of that issue that concerns the animal. Nonetheless it's important that I let them communicate what is on their mind rather than force an agenda on them.

In the case of Jasper, a black-and-white springer spaniel, I had been asked to find out how his medication for arthritis was working and whether he was coping all right with all of the veterinary involvement. But Jasper had a different worry about the same topic. *They're spending too much money on me,* he said, *and they can't afford it.* I knew there had been a lot of tests and investigations on Jasper before it had been confirmed that he did indeed have arthritis, and he was right – the treatment was both expensive and long-term. *It takes up so much of their time,* Jasper went on. *They take me to the vet, they are so good with my exercise and taking care of me, but I feel so guilty.* Jasper loved his human family so much, and all I could really do to console him was reassure him that they loved him too and would do anything for him. I suggested that the best thing he could do for them was to take his medication and do all that the vet suggested. The family wanted him with them for as long as possible and they would do anything they could to facilitate that.

Jasper, Sophie and Ozzy all taught me a great deal about the emotional complexities of animal behaviour, but they also taught me never to assume that I could anticipate just how any animal's story might evolve. A dog who was worried about money, a cat who was bored of being pampered, and a dog who had been living rough all had what we would think of as human experiences – for me, now, they are common animal experiences. We are animals too; and remembering that is to take the first step towards a better understanding of those with whom we share this world.

The sad lives many of them have led leave lingering feelings we could readily understand if we communicated with them.

I had sessions with a very moody mare called Fox – and thankfully her mum agreed with my description of her. She was such an angry horse, and not shy of vocalizing it. As is the case with many creatures, on deeper exploration it transpired that her anger was actually rooted in grief – she'd had no real 'foalhood' and had been worked, very heavy-handedly, from a young age until she shut down emotionally.

She was grieving for a lost childhood: *I want someone to love me, I want someone to love me for who I am, and I want to love back,* she told me, sadly, but she had never really expressed who she truly was, for she was so caught up in her grief – which she displayed in anger and moods. Fox didn't know how to take or give love, and that was her key problem.

Her mum described her as 'a time bomb waiting to go off', and desperately wanted to help her. After listening to Fox's tale (never underestimate the importance of listening) and empathising, she found it possible to change her temperament. As I was told: 'She's like a different horse, it really is quite amazing. We're now able to hack out without any nonsense or moodiness, and her eyes are so soft when we tell her how much we love her. It's beautiful – thank you so much.'

The changes in all of these animals were huge – and could be put down first and foremost to the animal feeling heard and understood, and secondly to the clearing of their grief. I was finally accepting that this was all real – and that I was genuinely making a difference.

Chapter 10

The Green-Eyed Monster

Some communicators believe that animals cannot feel negative or hurtful emotions such as jealousy – however, that is not my experience. Not only have I seen plenty of evidence to the contrary, but I also feel that to deny an animal any emotion at all is to place us right back in that dangerous time when we thought they felt nothing. Why should they be denied certain feelings? Animals have plenty of emotional scars and fears, and they have many ways of expressing them. As my experiences continued, I found out more and more about this aspect of animals' lives.

Creatures such as Dolly still carry that blueprint of trauma with them – she would never forget the agony of all those litters, or the pain as every puppy was taken away from her and she was forced to go through the whole process again. Many good and kind people take on rescue animals and do amazing work with them, but those animals have deep scars which sometimes can't help but break open. We must be patient and treat these creatures with love to help them heal and trust that the bad times have gone.

There are certainly animals who are envious of the attention that another animal or person gets from their mum or dad, or of the addition of a new companion into the life of the human they love. When that envy is combined with unhappy or cross feelings about something else in their life, you can expect trouble – and if it's a cat who's involved, even worse!

I dealt with one young feline whose name was Roule and she wasn't happy with that one little bit. *It's cheesy*, she told me – obviously she had a sense of humour, but she was making a serious point. Although she had a playful streak, she was absolutely certain that she wanted her name changed; she even knew what she wanted it changed to. *I want to be called Tara*, she said. When I asked her why, she told me, *That's a special name; it's what I was called before*. I told her I'd pass on her request to her dad, who had contacted me about her, but I was more concerned about the anger that was emanating from her. Roule or Tara was fed up and rather lethargic, but I also sensed that she was very strongly territorial and she felt that this territory was being invaded – hence her sadness.

What do you see as your territory, Tara? I asked her. *The flat*, she replied, *I really don't go out.* There was certainly no connection to outdoors, so this was consistent with what I was feeling. I knew she was the only cat in the family, which could only mean that she was having territorial issues with a person. I felt a very strong connection to the bedroom door and asked her whether that was an area she was allowed access to. She was hesitant but finally said, *Yes . . . I'm usually allowed in there.* Tara then showed me an image of the bedroom door being shut and flashed me the representation of a man – with that came more frustration, and some dislike. *Is that your dad? Is that Brian?* I asked. *No. No, it is not – I have my mum.* He *doesn't like me.* Ah! This was the heart of the matter – her mum, Catherine, had a new partner, and Tara was feeling left out. I knew that this was rather unfair – Brian was very fond of her, which was why he had contacted me – but I had to accept that this was all from the cat's perspective.

Why does he not let you into the bedroom? I asked.

No idea, she replied huffily.

When I reported back to Brian he confirmed that Tara was Roule's original name given to her by Catherine. They were both more than happy to call her Tara again. Interestingly, Brian said he felt Tara had taken a sudden dislike to him recently and neither he nor Catherine knew why. Brian actually suffered from asthma and Tara's hairs were making his attacks worse, which was why he closed the bedroom door: to avoid sleeping in an area in which she would be in all day, given half the chance. Whenever Tara got the opportunity she'd push the door open and roll around on the bed all day – it was only when Brian tried to sleep at night and found himself unable to because of his breathing difficulties that he and Catherine would realize what Tara had done again. She really was a very naughty girl.

Overall, I felt that Tara was really struggling at the moment and that this struggle was rooted in emotion. I needed to reassure her that there was room for three in the family. Her sadness was linked to her desire for things to go back to the way they were before Brian's arrival and was manifesting outwardly as anger. Unfortunately this anger was directed at Brian, as she saw him as the impetus for the change. I also picked up what I felt to be real issues of control and power. It felt like she was pleased that Catherine and Brian had been disagreeing or arguing about her. However, that was merely an indication of just how powerless she had been feeling, as well as of her belief that no one was listening to what she wanted.

When I had my next session with Tara, I brought up something that Brian had mentioned: there had been children visiting the flat and Tara had tried to scratch them. Catherine felt this was totally out of character and wanted to know why she had acted that way. It seemed obvious to me that it was simply another manifestation of Tara's upset and an attempt to get attention, but I checked with her. *I want to be left alone*, she told me. I asked what she meant, given that I knew the children hadn't been provoking her. *Catherine and Brian didn't see what they did.* She was certainly implying that the children had done something to provoke her, but I really felt this was a complete untruth. All animals can be economical with the truth, but I find cats more so than any other species (which makes my work very difficult at times), and I had to lay it on the line with her in terms of what could happen if she continued to attack children.

She wasn't happy. However, when I asked if she would allow me to do some clearing and grounding work with her, she was very open. I worked on her sense of security and, very interestingly, as soon as I had finished clearing off the heart and moved on to the throat, I felt a huge 'ball' lift from my own chest and then started to laugh for no reason. I felt sure that this was actually Tara laughing. She had a huge shift during the session and, all of a sudden, tears were rolling down my face – tears of old sadness accompanied by a feeling of relief and happiness. Tara clearly wanted to get better, and the fact that I had challenged her about what had happened with the children had made her see that she wasn't going to get away with anything, and that I was trying to do things for her own good.

I felt it was very important to give her back some control, so I asked Tara what she wanted. *I want Brian to leave me alone – I will go to him when I'm ready, and not a moment before*, she informed me. *And I want more one on one time with my mum!* She showed me an image of her and Catherine together, with her on her mum's lap, and a feeling of real intimacy. The physical shift I felt in my own body that day was the strongest I have ever experienced, and the physical power of what comes through to me via animals was best exemplified by that moment.

The next time I tuned in with her, she felt much lighter and with more positive energy. I asked her how things were with Brian. She hesitated for a moment (she was still the same aloof character!) before admitting: *Better – I want to be able to accept him. I'm getting there. Please ask them to be patient with me.*

Had it not been dealt with, the jealousy that Tara felt would have ultimately worked against her – had Brian continued to suffer asthma attacks despite having kept Tara out of the bedroom, as he and Catherine believed they had been, they may have re-homed Tara because they thought they had no alternative. Animals, like us, rarely see how their behaviour is making things worse for them when they are hurt and being ruled by their emotions so very strongly. As I said at the start of this chapter, I disagree with the idea that animals are full of nothing but love and are incapable of negative emotions. I find that animals do indeed experience the same full range of emotions that we do – and, as with ourselves, there is often an underlying issue that leads to bad behaviour, whether it's fear, insecurity or frustration.

These experiences were coming thick and fast when I was asked to communicate with Sally, a beautiful cross breed, because her loving guardian, Izzy, was worried as she had stopped coming into the bedroom at night – something she had always done. No encouragement would entice her in. Sally presented as a vocal, energetic dog with a real youthful vitality for life. She came over as loving and affectionate, but on deeper exploration of this she actually felt like quite an emotionally needy dog who demanded a lot of time and attention from Izzy. When I checked in with Sally on the subject of why she had stopped going into the bedroom, she wasn't shy about letting me know what had gone on. *Mum loves Hayley more than me*, she began. Hayley was Izzy's other dog and I knew that she had been very ill recently. *I feel left out. I feel sad. I don't like it.* Ah, she was making a stand. Sally's emotions were very childlike; she sounded like a sulking toddler who is thinking only of herself. I don't mean this in a bad way – love and concern for Hayley also came through – but the petulance was expressed with the egocentricity of a child who likes and expects things their own way all of the time. She was aggrieved because Hayley was old and less physically able: not only was she unable to play with her any more, but she was getting all the attention too.

Mum and Hayley don't want me in the bedroom – they want to be alone, she went on. I told Sally that this simply wasn't true. I pointed out that it wasn't every mum that would stand and cook her homemade meals every night, the way Izzy did for both her dogs. After I had reassured Sally and showed her the ways in which her mum demonstrated that she really did love her, she said that she was still going to stay out of the bedroom. I couldn't work that one out until she explained it to me. *I know Hayley has been really ill – and I know that she needs Mum. I'm going to let them have some time together*. What a lovely dog she actually was. Sometimes jealousy can be quite easily dealt with once the animal is given more information and a third party points out the obvious to them – in this case how much Izzy clearly loved *both* her dogs.

There have been instances when what has seemed like straightforward jealousy has actually been feelings based on what the animal wants for their human rather than for themselves. A beautiful boxer dog called Rory was angry towards and jealous of his mum's new partner, but his feelings were different to those of Sally. Rory didn't think this man was good enough for his mum, or even the right person for her to have in her life. He and the man had a mutual dislike of each other but that was actually irrelevant. *He's not right for my mum*, Rory said over and over. Yes, he was jealous, and yes, he wanted his mum to spend time with him, but he also sensed the latent anger of this man and was concerned as to whether he would become aggressive towards his mum. Although I did bring it up as sensitively as I could, Rory's mum was in the first flush of love and could see no wrong in her new partner. She chose to ignore Rory's warnings and put it all down to 'his nose being out of joint'. I wasn't at all convinced that this was an accurate assessment, but I can only do so much. I asked Rory to look out for his mum but to be careful – it was important that he stay in the home with her rather than be excluded and leave her unprotected.

The emotions of animals can be just as intense as ours and they have the same capacity as we do to overly attach themselves to another – even if it causes problems. Ebby, a wonderfully energetic, playful, desperate-to-please eight-month-old cocker spaniel was madly envious of anyone who came near her mum. To begin with when I communicated with her, all she would say was, *She's mine, she's mine, she's mine!* It was terribly hard to get past that. She kept telling me that she didn't want anyone else to touch her mum, and it wasn't until I had let her run out of steam telling me how much she loved her that we could even progress on to anything else at all.

One day I was at an event completely unrelated to animal communication when a woman casually mentioned to me that she had a cat, Charley, who was always being attacked by another cat, Dusty, who lived next door. This woman said that she didn't like Dusty at all and didn't know what to do to keep her from fighting with Charley. I wasn't working or tuned in, so thought that if any information did come through it would be for Charley – perhaps telling him how to protect himself. I was stunned when Dusty appeared – what a poor wee thing she was! She was indeed jealous of Charley entering her territory, but a little deeper exploration revealed that the jealousy was actually insecurity – she was so insecure and fearful that she needed to show this new cat who was boss. Once I explained this to Charley's mum, she was able to completely empathize and said she would go out of her way to pet and pay attention to little Dusty, who soon became a frequent, friendly visitor to their garden.

A similarly destructive emotion is anger. As soon as I

tuned in to a horse client called Jet, all I felt was anger. I had been asked to communicate with him as there had been changes in his behaviour that his mum simply couldn't understand. He was a big horse and becoming more and more dangerous. Further exploration identified that this anger was rooted in grief and an overwhelming sense of loss. While this was all being unpacked, he told me that he was lonely and misunderstood; I felt very much at this stage of the communication that the core of Jet's problem was rooted in anger and this was reinforced by imagery of him kicking out. However, while it was an image of him kicking outwards, it did seem to be more symbolic than literal: he was actually kicking out in anger. On trying to get to the root of what was making him angry I was receiving these images of him kicking out his back legs again and again. He said that he wanted to be left alone and he didn't like people around him or looking at him.

I asked whether he had always felt this angry, which was important because I was receiving feelings and sensations of him having previously been a placid, biddable horse who liked to please. I also felt that he could have been pushed quite far and this wouldn't have bothered him, yet he was so angry now.

I felt there had been a change of companion for Jet. A mate had left him and he was still grieving for him, even though this felt like a long time ago. It soon transpired that Jet had lost his field mate and was taking the anger out on his mum, who had removed his friend from the field and never returned him. It felt as though he had more recently had a new horse introduced into his world with the expectation that they would get on. It was this expectation that upset him and added to his anger: he was cross that it was assumed that he should be able to accept this new horse as a replacement for his old mate without being consulted. At this point I received very strong feelings of intrusion, territory, and the sense that the new horse could never replace his lost friend.

Interestingly, at this point Jet's anger suddenly started to dissipate and dissolved into overwhelming grief. It was now becoming clear that Jet had been grieving all this time for his lost friend and he was coping by turning his grief into anger. Unfortunately the anger was directed at his mum. This could be for one of two reasons: because he held her responsible for taking his mate away, or because his mum loved him and therefore he felt safest expressing his anger with her.

I asked Jet if he had any messages for me to pass on, and he most certainly did. *Tell Mum that I love her so much and I'm sorry.* I felt that, deep down, he knew that his anger towards her was unjustified and unreasonable. He showed me an image for his mum of him nuzzling his head right inside her jacket where she kept treats – he really liked this. It felt like this was an old behaviour but one that he wanted to get back to. *Please ask her to have patience with me.* This is often a concern for animals: they feel that they will run out of time with us if they continue to do 'naughty' things, but they often don't know how else to express themselves or make the changes they so desire. *I want some time with her alone – without any of the other horses. Can you ask her that for me? I know none of this is her fault.* There was a sense of sadness at the realization of how he had been behaving but also a sense of excitement and lightness at the prospect of everything being better between him and his mum, and indeed the relationship did get back to normal once his behaviour improved after my sessions with him.

These emotions are no different to the ones we feel – but, while we can shout, and we can tell people how we feel, animals have to hope that someone will open the door to communicating with them. Once I passed information on to Jet, he felt much better simply by seeing the 'whole picture' – many people don't tell animals what is happening and, without knowledge, the animal may worry unnecessarily. We chatter away quite happily to our pets quite often, but I do think we should talk about the things that affect them too, rather than just use them as a repository for our own worries. I often wonder how many poor creatures have been abandoned, rehoused or even put to sleep simply because the real reasons for their behaviours were misunderstood. It's up to all of us to pay attention to what the creatures who share our lives may be telling us, and to give them the respect they deserve.

It was simply a miracle that all of these animals were

coming into my life, generously sharing their stories and their experiences with me, when, not so long before, I had had no idea that such encounters even existed. At this point, I had so much to thank Dan for – little did I know that the most important teacher of my life was just waiting to contact me.

Chapter 11

My New Teacher

Barney the border collie was my biggest teacher. Dan changed my life but Barney changed my approach: he was the dog I learned from most. Dan may have opened the door but Barney did so much more. He was a wise old soul whose mum wanted to know if he was happy and if there was anything she could do to improve his life. When Claire first came to me about him I had no idea that he would come to mean so much to me, or that I could possibly learn such a great deal from one animal. What I did comprehend very quickly was that Barney's role here in this world was actually to be a wonderful teacher.

All animals like to see themselves as having jobs, whether that's as a guard dog or a cat whose mum relies on her to speak to at the end of a horrible day at work. I firmly believe, as did he, that Barney was put on this earth to teach and pass on his amazing knowledge. Claire was a dog trainer and loved animals, but, being analytical, logical and solution-focused in her approach to work, she was also a bit of a sceptic, and completely unsure as to whether anyone could communicate with her dog, which is why I actually reverted to a way of working that

I hadn't done since my early days as a pet whisperer. I told Claire that I was quite happy to ask Barney a series of questions that only Claire would know the answers to. When I reported back all of the information to her with accuracy, she was staggered – and an immediate convert. As a result, Claire felt assured and confident in the work Barney and I did, improving her understanding of him and, therefore, benefitting their relationship. Claire was actually much more open than she gave herself credit for, but I was happy to go along with proving myself to her as it would have been counter-productive to pass on messages from her dog if her scepticism had never been addressed.

Barney was serious, an intense character with a determined nature, but he also possessed a real gentleness, accompanied by a regal, stately air. The first thing I said to him was, *You're really handsome* – to which he said, *I know*. This wasn't conceit, it was fact. Claire said she and her husband told him this all the time and she recognized his character straight away. I asked permission to do a body scan on Barney and told him that his mum wanted me to ask some questions on her behalf – my immediate impression of Barney was that very little would surprise him. He was patient and understanding, and I felt like a novice in his presence. I asked him what his favourite toy was, and what games he liked, and I received images of a multi-coloured ball and a Frisbee, which Claire later confirmed as accurate, but when I asked him what he liked to do I got an image of him lying on a sofa. Not very exciting! I could tell he was an old dog (he was actually only seven years old, though his 'real' age was much more than this), but was that really his most favourite pastime? *Well*, he began cautiously, *you see, I'm not really meant to go on that sofa.* Ah! He liked it so much because it was forbidden. I then asked him where in the house was his favourite place to lie, and I heard a deep sigh. *I've already told you that*, he said, in a really slow, resigned voice, sending me the image of him on the sofa again. *Sorry*, I sent back. Lesson one: pay attention to the information given and don't bother the animal with the same question in different ways unless it's vitally important! There was no way Barney would have been lying to me about the sofa, because he was confiding something that was naughty. *Actually, Barney*, I said, *I think your mum knows you go on the 'banned' sofa.* I had got a really strong sense of Claire's amusement when Barney sent me the image for the second time. *I know she does*, he said, *but I'm just not quick enough*. What did that mean? He sent me an image of himself lying on the sofa and then jumping off as soon as he heard Claire coming downstairs. I later found out that they had wooden floors which gave him away and Claire could always hear his nails click as he launched himself off the sofa; the fact that he was arthritic also meant that the whole business was a bit of a performance for him, and certainly not one that he could do quietly. He asked me not to tell his mum about him on the sofa. It was only during Claire's feedback on my findings that she mentioned that he liked to lie on the sofa. True to my word, I kept quiet and later tuned in to Barney to tell him she definitely knew. *I know*, he said resignedly and gave me permission to give her the story. We had a laugh about it.

I asked him what his favourite walk was but all I got was an image of one that I often went on with my own dog, Lady. *Do you go there too, Barney?* I asked. *No*, he replied. I asked him again to send me the image of his favourite walk, and back came the same image. I was confused. *Is that the walk you'd like to go on?* I asked him, even though I knew he didn't live anywhere near me. *No, try again*, he told me, once more sending the same image. I sat back and thought about it – what was he trying to tell me? I had no doubt that this clever dog could send me whatever he wanted, so why was he keeping this image going when it was clearly a walk he had no experience of? It was a river walk, with lots of trees, and the noise of soft, running water in the background. *Do you go on a walk like that somewhere else, Barney?* I asked, the penny finally dropping. *Yes, yes, I do.* Ah, that was it – he had sent me an image of a walk that I knew well because, while I wouldn't be familiar with his own favourite walks, I would recognize the key elements of my own walk. Lesson two: animals often send you something that is personal and familiar to you in order that you can understand and make sense of it and then work out how it applies to them.

I then asked him if he had a secret – again, this was

something I had learned from the workshop days, but by this point it wasn't something I tended to rely on. In fact, I'm now a little uneasy about that phrase, as there's something about *secrets* that doesn't sit comfortably with me, but I will always ask if there's something the animal I'm working with wants to share. Barney showed me a tap-dancing stick, the sort that someone like Fred Astaire would use, and with it came an overwhelming sense of being at school. There were lots of little kids with their hands up, saying, *Me, me, me, choose me!* And an equally overwhelming sense of joy, love, happiness and excitement all around. I didn't know what it meant. Then Barney showed me what looked like Crufts and what I thought was a dog ring – though in fact it transpired that there was a fairly new craze to do heelwork to music with dogs and that was what Barney was indicating. When I asked whether he enjoyed it he didn't respond with a *yes*, just the sense of *Next time choose me*. I fed back to Claire and said I had no idea what any of this meant – it was Barney's secret and it had something to do with dancing and music and some association with Crufts, and he really wanted to do it. 'Oh my goodness,' she said, 'I do heelwork to music with Clyde, my other dog, but never with Barney – I'd never thought he would like it.'

Barney also shared with me that he didn't really see the point in dog training – *She tells me to sit, lie, stand, stay. What's the purpose? I know how to do all these things. What's the point?* – which made her laugh. 'Have you ever met a dog trainer with a dog she can't use? He won't do any-thing in class, even though he's so well-behaved – he just can't be used as a subject.' I wasn't surprised – I knew Barney.

I asked Barney if he was happy and he said, *Yes, ecstati-cally so – I don't want to be anywhere else.* I had certainly felt happiness and contentment coming from him, but he was still evading my request to do a body scan. I asked again and he was very uncertain. I reassured him and said we could stop whenever he wanted to and he gave me permission to proceed. He was in a lot of pain, from what I could tell, but as soon as I thought that he inter-rupted: *No, no pain.* I found this hard to believe. *Are you sure?* I asked. *No pain, just a bit sore, sometimes stiff and tender.* Lesson three: some animals will react strongly to words that they feel are wrong for their character. Barney was such a stoical dog that what would have been pain for another animal was something he described only as 'a bit sore'. I also sensed that he didn't want to scare Claire, so was underplaying the physical aches he had. It was very obvious to me that Barney had arthritis in the hips, as the area felt crumbly and bony – I had never felt bone like that before and I just knew it was arthritis. Learning how to feel bone and identify arthritis was an important development for me. Claire confirmed that he had hip dysplasia which had developed into debilitating arthritis and said that his pain (her choice of word) and discomfort were often clearly visible and, at his worst, he had to be lifted up and downstairs, and carried outside to the toilet.

The most interesting thing about Barney's body scan and one of the biggest learning points was when he drew me into his arthritic back legs with a magnetic pull. I asked him which was worse, his left or his right. We went round the houses for twenty minutes – *Which is worse?* He pulled me into the right. *OK, your right hip is most painful?* I said. *No,* he replied. *So, which is more painful?* I asked. *Left.* I was confused. *Your left one's worse?* He didn't get cross as he said, *No. Right.* We went round in circles about this for what seemed like forever. I thought I was doing it all wrong so I stopped, took a few deep breaths and went back in. *How do we work out the hip thing? Which hip is worse?* I asked. *Right.* That was clear enough. *Which hip is the most painful?* I checked. *Left.* Got it! The right was the most deteriorated, so it was in the worst physical state, but the left was giving him more pain. Another lesson duly noted, this one number four: be absolutely explicit, be clear and always check things out.

However, when I relayed my findings to Claire she told me I wasn't correct – Barney's left hip was the most affected. I groaned, as it had taken so long to work it out, but she phoned back later to say I was right: after our conversation she'd checked the X-rays; they provide a mirror image of the skeleton and that's what had confused her.

I also felt that Barney was very sore around the stomach area, and asked him if this was the case. When he said it was, I asked if it was always sore. *No, just with the baby.* But Barney was a male dog. He certainly hadn't given birth, but as soon as I thought this, he sent me images of Claire. I was sure she must be pregnant and that Barney was feeling her discomfort.

Barney pulled me back to his arthritis so I asked, *What would help you, Barney?* Immediately I got flashes of yellow coming through. I asked if he would like a yellow blanket. *Yes.* I asked if he would like some yellow food. *Yes.* With that came an image of some potatoes. He kept sending it to me, with enormous patience, until I finally clicked that the vegetables were in fact yellow peppers, not potatoes. The images of yellow just kept coming in waves. He seemed very sure that he wanted this colour but I couldn't work out why, as blue is traditionally the colour of healing and I felt this would be much more appropriate for him.

I had been with Barney for quite some time and I was really enjoying it, but I was exhausted. He didn't always answer my questions directly, instead preferring to have me unpack things and work for what I was getting. He really did seem very wise and tolerant – and was teaching me lots! I had another session with him a few days later, and did some distance-healing work with him in the interim. After giving my feedback to Claire, she said that her main concern was related to the arthritis medication Barney was being given. She wanted to know what he thought of it and whether he was getting the right treatment.

Naturally Barney's hip problems meant that he could no longer run the way he'd used to with his dog companion, Clyde, and this, Claire felt, was affecting his mood. He was spending long periods of time sleeping and was receiving daily pain relief. She was looking for a long-term solution to the problem and wanted to know what was helping. I sent him images of liquid medication, syringes and tablets. I didn't know what pain relief Barney was on so asked him if he was on medication and if it helped. He told me that he needed the white ones speckled with brown but that the other ones weren't doing anything, but he also sent yellow, yellow, yellow again. I still hadn't worked out the significance of that. Although I completely trusted that he knew what was good for him, I couldn't grasp why he was consistently choosing yellow for himself. I told him that he had got me thinking and that I was going to do some research into the benefits of the colour yellow. I then realized he was doing the doggy, psychic equivalent of raising his eyebrows at me. Of course! Why do research when I could just ask Barney? So I did.

Stimulation without aggravation.

Stimulation without aggravation.

Stimulation without aggravation.

How amazing. Yellow stimulates but is much gentler than orange or red, which increase energy but I wouldn't use in case the arthritis or inflammation was aggravated. He was so clever! Lessons five and six: listen to what the animal sends you repeatedly, and realize that they have a great deal of wisdom that we can access. I did indeed send him lots of yellow and Claire gave him a yellow blanket for his dog bed – this was a bed in which he had never spent a single night in all of his seven years, but that night he trotted over to it and slept there until morning. He clearly needed to absorb the gentle yellow energy, and that's why he'd repeatedly asked for it.

Claire said that she'd noticed a major improvement in Barney after the first session and the course of therapy work I'd been doing. The stiffness in his joints was no longer noticeable and he seemed to have regained much of the power in his back legs. This was incredible. I mentioned the stomach discomfort to her and she told me that, yes, she was pregnant. I was 100 per cent sure that was the answer to that area of discomfort for Barney – he was mirroring her symptoms, which is common practice between animals and humans who are close. In fact, when Claire next brought Barney back to my treatment room, she said she was concerned about his perineum area, which as she had noticed was quite red and sore-looking. I intuitively asked her how her own perineum was and she advised me that she had just seen her doctor for her six-week postnatal check – and had her episiotomy stitches removed. She said that her pain had gone the day she noticed Barney's perineum looking red and sore. We talk about our animals mirroring things but they can take our pain too. Claire's pain and inflammation in that area of her body was clearly – visibly – being carried by Barney.

My sessions with Barney were remarkable and I will never be able to thank him enough for what he gave to me – sadly, my time knowing him on this earth was all too short. He came here to teach and teach he did; he left when his job was done.

Chapter 12

Barney's Talent

Before Barney crossed the rainbow bridge, he left me with lessons that have influenced and changed the way in which I work with animals. When Claire brought Barney to me for healing sessions I was delighted to find that my experience with Dan was not to be repeated with my new doggy guide. He was a beautiful dog, with a gentle, loving nature that was completely in tune with the patient client I knew. I believe that some animals, like people, are more evolved than others and I knew that Barney fitted into that category. His role was to be a teacher and, although his physical condition caused him great pain, I know that the information he gave me about other things he wanted, including the medication that worked for him and the joy of dancing to music with his mum, meant that his last months were as comfortable and fulfilled as they could be. He was meant to be a challenge to me and to Claire, to open doors and to leave this wonderful legacy.

Barney was so easy to work with in the flesh, too – although I generally didn't work in person with clients, it was different with him. He was happy to be there and I felt it was part of his teaching strategy. Any time he moved he moved for my benefit, to show me a part of his body that needed work or to indicate that it was time to move to the next area. He would roll over just at the time I needed to work on the other side. Again this was about him being the teacher: *This is how you do it; this is where to work; this is when to stop working . . .* He very much led me through it. After three one-to-one healing sessions with him, he was off his painkillers. It was actually accidental that Claire hadn't given them to him – I got in touch a fortnight after the sessions ended, to follow up on how he was doing, and she said that for the last few days she'd forgotten to give him them; apparently he simply wasn't looking for them. Previously she had given them to him because she had seen that he was in so much pain which served as a reminder to her – without that reminder, she'd let it slip her mind. She didn't have that trigger any more, as his movements were so much more fluid and he was able to comfortably run around with Clyde again.

Sadly, Barney passed over eight months after we found each other. I knew he had been well, then suddenly unwell, so when Claire called to say that she'd had to have him put to sleep, I wasn't surprised. She asked me to tune in and see if she had done the right thing. As soon as I tuned in the energy felt really good; it was light, fluffed-up and buoyant. Barney told me that he felt wonderful, that he had no pain, and he also showed me a moving video of his passing. There was a man with him who meant a lot, but I couldn't see his mum. He showed me how he had received an injection between the shoulder blades. I remembered what Barney had taught me and knew this may not be what he wanted me to take literally – this was the only place in which I'd ever seen a dog injected, so it may have been a symbolic image to demonstrate that he had received a jab. Barney had already left the earth plane by the time the injection was administered and I got a feeling of relief from him. He was ready to go when it happened and he confirmed that it was indeed the right decision to make. *I was in pain – it was time. My purpose had been served.* I asked how Claire had coped with being there at the vet and he said that she couldn't go – she was too upset – and that was why I couldn't see her in the picture. He showed me imagery that denoted him as a teacher to both myself and Claire, saying that not only had he been ready to go, but also that his family had been ready to let him pass. This was important to him; I knew it had made it so much easier for Barney, for which he was grateful.

There was an energy drop when I asked him how Clyde was coping without him, which indicated the grieving that the other dog was going through, but he then told me he would *sort it out.* I had no doubt that he would – as well as being a formidable teacher, he was also marvellous at making sure everyone did what they were meant to do. Barney had said enough for one day, and wanted to leave – his final message was that he was watching over everything and everyone. I didn't want to close off – I wanted to stay with this wonderful creature – but I knew that he was teaching me still: it was up to the animal to end things when he or she wanted to, and I had to respect that.

I had to admit that, two days later, I returned to Barney. I just couldn't keep away. There was a clear message as soon as I tuned in: *Tell Claire that she is strong and she will get through this.* I felt that Claire must have been going through a period of uncertainty as these words were spoken. Barney said that I shouldn't worry about him, that he was *light, free and able to go on and do good work.* This was all about him continuing to be a teacher and he once more showed me the image of him passing over, to emphasize continuity. As he had moved towards the bright light, he said, *Gus was there to meet me.* He took me with him as he ran over a field towards this other dog, and a flooding of pure ecstasy washed over me. I felt so privileged to experience the sheer joy of him being free of pain and returning to his maker with his best friend. I always feel both honoured and humbled to be granted permission to engage in such intimate and emotional moments.

I had a smile on my face when he told me about Gus, because that was something he had already prepared me for. Back in the first communication with him he had shown me a white West Highland terrier and I hadn't known what the image meant. It was a statue rather than an actual dog, and all I could think was that a friend of mine had an ornament like that. I mentioned it in feedback, and Claire said they had nothing like that. I said it felt like this dog was in spirit, but she'd never had a Westie. We puzzled it and I thought I was just wrong. It had clearly been on Claire's mind because she phoned me the next day and asked if I was the one who knew a Westie. How could I have missed it? There was one next door to me, Angus. Claire laughed and said, 'That must be it – it's funny, because we had a dog years ago called Angus who we always called Gus.' Barney had been teaching me again: it hadn't been about a Westie – it had been about the name, and he was giving me clues to follow. Yet another lesson: when, after he passed, he again gave me the name Gus, I knew this was his best friend patiently waiting for him so that they could run free together again.

Again, I found it hard to go, but Barney told me that our time was up and that he would send me something so I would know that he was always watching over me. He wasn't forgetting Claire, either, as she would soon find out.

Exhausted, I fell asleep, my mind and dreams full of Barney. When I woke up, it was sunset and a feeling of peace was covering me. For some reason, I reached over to grab a pen and notebook from the side of the bed, where I always keep them (just in case) and found myself scribbling furiously. Now, I'm no poet, and I've never even tried before, but the words just came automatically. I had to write them down immediately, as if Barney was dictating an entire poem to me. This is what appeared:

An Ode to the Incredible Barney

Barney had definitely been here before, a soul both
wise and old.

Intense, determined, yet gentle too, caring for all in his
fold.

He took being a collie seriously, and liked to count or
herd.

Sheep, or balls or Frisbees – of his manor he was laird.

His role on earth was to teach, and this he clearly did;

How to talk to animals, without thinking you'd flipped
your lid!

Now Barney had two sore hips and said he needed
yellow.

Improvement and pain relief did follow, oh what a
wise old fellow.

Dog training was a waste of time, he'd done it all before.

'What's the point of all of that?' was the question at his
core.

He liked the look of heelwork – but to music it must be.

'Oh Mum,' he gently pleaded, 'next time, please choose
me.'

He had a little secret he wasn't keen to share.

He liked to lie on the sofa, when no one else was there.

He thought that he was crafty and had it all sussed too,

But pretty soon admitted that mum already knew.

His time was short, just seven years, but what a time
he had.

Walks and talks and lots of love, the best a dog could
    have.

The time and decision both were right, he reached out
    for the light.
His old friend Gus was waiting – what a wondrous
    sight.
Now he's there, light and well, of that please have no
    doubt.
Barney's doing what he does best – sorting us all out.

I clearly wasn't going to challenge the Poet Laureate
with my words, but what amazed me was that they
were even there in the first place. I've never written or
attempted poetry since, and I'm not surprised – those
weren't my lines, they were completely inspired by
Barney.

Claire and I had become friends by this time and I
quickly typed out the poem and posted it to her, excitedly
hoping she would like it. Claire adored the poem because
she felt that it was something Barney himself had written.
One day, several years later, Claire phoned me terribly
upset and said she'd 'acquired' a new dog. A little girl had
brought the dog to her for training and, somehow, she
just knew she had to have him. However, she said she
was in a mess because she'd lied to her husband about
how she'd got him.

As soon as she said it, I asked, 'Wait a minute – is your
dog called Ben?'

She repeated it back to me, questioningly. 'Ben?'

I must have got it wrong, I thought. 'Sorry,' I said, 'I've been doing admin, so I'm not tuned in for working.'

'It's funny you should say Ben: he used to be Ben but I've called him Goose.' As soon as she said it, Ben came straight in like a thunderbolt. 'Oh no,' I told her, 'you can't call him Goose – he's mortified!' He was saying to me, *There's no way she's calling me that; there's no way I'm answering to that daft name.* Claire laughed and said that she'd been calling him that for the last three days and he was ignoring her.

Claire's new dilemma was that her husband had told her there were too many dogs and that, if she wanted to keep Ben/Goose, one of the others had to go. She didn't know what to do. 'It's Henry,' I told her. She said she felt it should be 'last dog in, first dog out' but I knew immediately that she wasn't right. 'No,' I said, 'it's Henry who has to go.' I was sensing this very strongly (the claircognisance working its magic again) and I didn't need to check out the other animals and ask questions; it was clear that Henry had to be the one to leave. Claire adored Henry but she said that, as much as she loved him, she could rehome him much more easily than she could the other two. I knew, without thinking, without analysing or asking, the fact was there in my head: *Ben's meant to be with you.* 'What age is he?' I asked.

'He's a puppy,' she told me.

'I bet he doesn't have a puppy's bounciness,' I said, 'he's a steady Eddie.'

'Yes, he is,' she confirmed.

This new dog felt so much like Barney. He had the same old head on young shoulders, the same serious approach to life. I felt Barney – but could that possibly be the case? Was the spirit of Barney actually in Ben? Could this really be what had happened? It seemed incredible, almost unbelievable, but I had learned that so many things I would have previously discounted were not as bizarre as I may have thought. I didn't want to say to Claire, 'That's Barney back', and get her upset, but I did say that Ben/ Goose felt the way that Barney felt: really strong and dependable. She told me that was exactly how the new dog seemed to her. Claire explained to me that as soon as she saw him she knew she had to have him. My claircognisance was kicking in big time and I was getting shivers down my spine as we spoke. My wariness was disappearing and I really felt that Barney *was* here, that he was around and had come back to her. I was just beginning to understand how animals return to us and how strong our drive to have some pets in our lives can be.

I will always have a special place in my heart for the wonderful Barney, and the lessons he taught me have been absolutely invaluable. What I learned most was that animals are so often the best experts to turn to when we need guidance in terms of what to do to help them. They *know* what they need, be that food, exercise, colours, medication or therapy. While even the most sceptical of guardians accept things eventually through a mixture of love and proof, I find that animal professionals are less open. It's frequently the case that vets who have seen the most amazing things happen with creatures they know well will, with their last breath, nonetheless deny the possibility of other forces. Barney taught me to have faith in what animals tell me and in what I can do for them.

With a black Labrador puppy called Tyson it was difficult, for what human companion would be willing to stand up to a vet who was adamant that their way was the only way? Thankfully, Tyson's mum was made of stern stuff.

Tyson was brought to me with incredible pain in his front right leg caused by bilateral elbow osteoarthritis. He was unable to walk without limping. The poor thing was on huge amounts of pain relief and an operation seemed to be the only way forward for him. His mum, Maureen, was incredibly concerned about that option and was feeling under huge pressure, the vet having bluntly told her, 'If you love your dog you will make sure he has this operation, otherwise he won't be able to walk by the time he is two years old.'

Animal communication work identified that Tyson would suffer incredible separation anxiety as a result of being away from his brother, who depended on him hugely for emotional support. In view of the severity of this case, we decided that an immediate course of four daily therapy sessions would be the best way to start. The first treatment was carried out there and then in my treatment room, but the remainder were to be carried out as distance healing, given that the family lived quite far from me. After the first session, Maureen was thrilled that Tyson was limp-free and playing with his doggy friends quite happily.

However, the next day, she called rather upset and disappointed because the limp had returned. I assured her that this was a normal part of the healing process and it was the body adjusting to the new energy flow. I carried out further treatments that day and the following two days. The vet was aware of the work I was doing with Tyson and I advised Maureen to discuss pain relief with him, as Tyson was already intimating that he wouldn't need it for much longer. Over the course of two months his pain relief was gradually reduced while I worked on increasing the energy flow to his front legs. Very soon he reached the point where not only did he no longer require pain relief but also an operation wasn't necessary either.

Interestingly, the vet did not respond to my letters to him, nor did he take up the invitation to a free place on my Animal Communication Workshop; according to my client, he put Tyson's recovery down to my work having a 'placebo effect'. Tyson was a clever pup, but as to the placebo effect working on animals . . . Just exactly how is that possible? The energy treatments either work or they don't – an animal isn't going to think that he will be better because some strange woman is waving her hands around him!

I understand that for some vets my work is completely out of their experience. When I get frustrated for the animals about such closed attitudes, I simply bring the grace and presence of the magnificent Barney into my world to centre me – and I thank him yet again.

Chapter 13

Secrets and Desires

The work I did with Easta, the chestnut mare, was revealing because it really brought home to me the way in which animals have and keep secrets – sometimes ours, sometimes their own.

As soon as I tuned in with Easta I received the word 'beautiful'. She was clearly told this a lot and it was important to her. With Easta, my feedback included the following: 'Easta is drawing me into her front legs very strongly when I do the body scan. There was a considerable amount of pain there and it had been ongoing for quite some time.' I also had the strangest sensation of bumps/spots around my face when first tuning in with Easta. It didn't feel like a rash, just like bumpy skin. It was quite strange and like nothing I've ever experienced before – quite bizarre, really.

Her mum, Sarah, then told me: 'Easta was a pretty successful show jumper before I retired her two years ago. At that time, she had an inflamed deep digital flexor tendon in her left fore and an enlargement on her right tendon, again foreleg. I decided to retire her as I didn't want her to end up crippled for life if she continued to jump. She has recently cut her eye open quite badly – it has almost healed, but it looked pretty horrific at the time.'

Now, the medical terminology is often gobbledegook to me. I have no physiological knowledge of horses whatsoever, and I have chosen not to change that – not out of pride or obstinacy but because I've had clients who have said they actually prefer that I'm . . . well, ignorant about horse terms. One yard owner said she felt reassured by my lack of equine knowledge, as I awkwardly pointed to the areas of the horse's body to which I was being drawn, using human terminology to explain what I was finding i.e. elbows, wrists, waist etc. As she had previously engaged a number of experts to look at this horse, my lack of equine language and knowledge highlighted for her that I was genuinely giving her what I found, rather than reaching a conclusion based on the horse's physical presentation and medical background. Certainly when Easta's mum, Sarah, told me the specific physical problems the horse had, I could only relate them to what I had found. Ah, I thought – this is the soreness in her front legs that she pulled me towards. Similarly, the reference to her eye injury being 'horrific' to look at when it first occurred was a reference to the 'bumpy skin' I had been sent a sensation of.

On first reading, I intuitively felt that Easta had two personalities, and I picked up the potential for attention-seeking behaviour. She loved lots of attention and I could imagine that she could be prone to naughtiness if she didn't get the attention she needed and liked. This was all confirmed by Sarah: 'Easta is an outgoing, precocious youngster, very bold – she doesn't give a damn about anything. She is actually what I'd call a split personality; she loves to be the centre of attention.' I certainly felt she was a headstrong horse who knew what she wanted; and yet, while this strong, powerful personality was coming through clearly, I was also picking up what felt like shyness or fear. The more I explored this, the more I felt Easta to be a horse who experienced fearfulness and anxiety in certain situations. I had the distinct impression of her as horse of two contrasting natures. Sarah said: 'Sometimes as I work with her she will freak and get very scared.'

There was one thing I couldn't quite understand – Easta kept sending me a word that didn't make sense. The closest I could get was 'Pirelli', like the tyres. As hard as I tried to unpack it, I couldn't make sense of it at all, but it was something that Easta kept returning to and seemed to be important to her. I knew she appreciated something to do with this word, as I felt joy when she thought of it, but I was stuck. I also knew from images she had sent me that, somewhere in her past, she had experienced heavy handling, and I felt there was some sort of link between this and the word – but I couldn't work out why something good would be linked with something bad. When I got Sarah's response, all became clear – it was my horse ignorance again! 'I should point out that I am currently studying for my Parelli instructor assessments and Easta is only worked using natural-horsemanship methods. I started her that way and, as far as I can tell, she may have experienced other training in the past with whips and spurs, which I would never use. Due to the past training, her inbuilt flight mechanism kicks in with her and she will go from inquisitive and happy to fear/flight mode very quickly. I would say her "bad" behaviour is definitely fear-driven. She then gets snappy and has a tendency to rear, which again illustrates the extremes in her personality.'

Parelli was a new word for me – and had nothing to do with tyres. It made sense: Easta still had bad memories of training that had been abusive, but she appreciated what Sarah was trying despite having no control over the memories it dredged up for her. Communicating with me about her past – and probably also feeling frustration that I didn't understand everything – had an effect on Easta and, although incredibly chatty when I tuned in and clearly happy to communicate lots of information to me, she decided halfway through to clam up. It was like pulling teeth after that, but I felt a couple of different things could be at play here. I wondered if this was indicative of her personality. As I'd later found out, she was showing two very different natures, demonstrating real contrast between them. I also felt that we had touched a raw nerve at one point when, very briefly, the loss of a partner or field mate came up. This felt old and hadn't happened while she was with Sarah, but it still hurt her. I felt that

Easta was a horse who needed time to build trust and relationships, and I was glad that I still had another session left with her.

Easta was incredibly responsive to the therapy work I did in between our communications and it was a real pleasure working on her, but when I returned I found her to be quiet and reserved. She wasn't uncommunicative, just more pensive and reticent. Some further exploration confirmed that she indeed had something on her mind – our previous session had made her move towards making an important decision. Sarah emailed me to say that she was thinking of giving Easta the chance to have a foal – not to sell but to keep with her – and she wanted me to use the session to check out how Easta felt about this. Before I had even finished reading the email, the information was there: *YES, YES, YES!* She would *love* to have a foal to keep! That part of the communication was incredibly emotional and I felt all weepy. It was beautiful and such a privilege to share that incredibly intimate moment of 'woman to woman' communication with her. She then went on to talk to me about her 'job'. I wondered what she could mean and why she was moving the focus away from the idea of having a foal, which had seemed to make her so happy. She said she *needed* a job – something meaningful to do. When I asked her what she might like as her employment she said, *To be a mother*, which made sense. I felt the time was right for Easta to have that role. Being a mother is the most important job of all, she felt, and she wanted it. I also sensed that motherhood might help settle this sense of fear which she displayed, this edgy side to her personality.

I want to be with my foal, she told me. *Please don't let anyone separate us.* I was able to reassure her that Sarah's plan was for her to stay with the foal forever, and not to sell it. Despite the very strong maternal feelings Easta was sending me, I also knew she would not be an over-protective mother. She was an independent horse and wanted her foal to be so too. Easta told me she would be a good mum. *I will make Sarah proud.* Again, this was so moving and emotional. She clearly desired her own foal very much and wanted to do the best job she could. This was something that made me want to cry again. I felt a very strong male presence around the potential foal, and was so glad that Easta was going to get what she wanted: a choice that we humans often take for granted but that animals are often denied.

When I asked her if she had any preference regarding who the father of her foal should be, she sent me the word *dark*. This was followed by an image of a black horse. This horse had a strong personality coupled with a real gentle side to his nature, and Easta felt very emotional about him when she sent me the picture. I knew that she needed this horse to be the father and I passed the information on.

Recently, I contacted Sarah to ask permission to use Easta's story in this book (she thought Easta's diva side would love the publicity!) and took the opportunity to ask how things had gone with the foal. My heart sank as I read the email: 'After much deliberation, I chose a handsome black stallion for Easta, but when the time came he wasn't available. So, I chose a lovely quarter horse stallion, a cremello colour. Easta absolutely loved him and they were inseparable for two months. However, she got an infection very early on in her pregnancy and miscarried, so no foal. We're now waiting until next year to try once more, although I am now undecided over the quarter horse again or using the black stallion.' I pray that they decide to go with the black horse that Easta wanted so badly – the miscarriage was no doubt nature's way of dealing with things, and Easta's health was the priority, but I do dearly wish for her dream of becoming a mother to come true and I know that Sarah will do whatever it takes to ensure that the light of her life gets what she wants and needs. The rest, of course, is down to nature.

The secrets that animals hold can surprise all of us – who would have thought that a horse would have such strong views on motherhood and on the potential father of her foal? – but they can also tell us or draw our attention to things that we simply don't consciously realize, or deliberately want to ignore. When I worked with one cat, Tammy, I was shocked by the dislike she had of her mum's partner. The guardians had only recently begun sharing a house together, and I immediately suspected that Tammy was feeling a little put out at having to share her mum.

However, the more she spoke and the more images she sent, the more I felt it was deeper than that. She loved her mum so much and said that she only wanted the best for her. When I asked what that would involve, Tammy said: *She has to get rid of him. He's no good for her – all he does is take.* These words were accompanied by some very strong images of the couple: generic male and female figures arguing, with the female being very upset when the man left the scene. This, in turn, upset Tammy, and she had no hesitation in calling the man a range of colourful names. She was adamant that I *had to tell* her mum – but what could I do? Is it my place to inform people that their animal companions sometimes allow me to see the most intimate details of their lives, albeit from their perspective? Yes, I think it is my place to say something if it's important enough for the animal to share with me and it is causing them upset; it is my job to be their voice. I have learned to couch my words sensitively and always remind guardians that I speak from the animal's perspective, not a place of judgement. Indeed, sometimes things are too awful even for the animal to continue looking at. When I worked with Philip the dog, he seemed such a happy, bouncy chap – but it was all a carefully constructed façade, hiding the horror of domestic violence he had witnessed for years. The images of abuse that he sent me were heartbreaking, as was his recognition that he couldn't do what he most wanted to – which was to attack his mum's abuser – as there was a chance he would be sent away, and he knew that his most important job was to provide her with love and affection. I had only one session with Philip, and, even though when I fed back to his mum I was incredibly tactful and sensitive, barely scratching the surface of what Philip told me, I often wonder whether it had hit a raw nerve, because she never came back.

Animals cannot possibly understand all of the complications and strange aspects of human life, just as we don't comprehend all of their experiences, but there are certain things that must bewilder them totally. Sadly, one such thing is the effects of alcohol. The way in which humans change, often not for the better, after drinking is something dogs in particular see the consequences of all too frequently.

Buddy the golden retriever presented as a regal, stately dog who was only a youthful four years old but had an old head on him. I described him as a 'pipe and slippers by the fire' sort of dog, which made his guardian laugh as that was exactly how he was. Buddy was a bit of a worrier, a purposeful creature who seemed to be taking on a lot. I felt like he had quite a weight on his young shoulders. He told me, *Life is serious*.

It transpired that his dad, Roger, was quite a heavy drinker who self-harmed when he used alcohol. Buddy felt that he needed to protect Roger from himself when he drank; he also said, *There's something else, something that I'm not sure if I should tell.* It is always up to the animal to decide whether or not to disclose, just as it had always been up to the vulnerable adults and teenagers I once worked with. Nevertheless I did all I could to make Buddy feel that he was in a supportive, trusting environment so that he would feel safe to share his worries with me.

Eventually he did.

Dad hits Mum, he whispered. *I need to protect him but I need to protect her too. I don't like when he drinks that stuff – it changes him, he doesn't seem like my dad. He isn't nice to us, he isn't nice to Chester.* Chester was the other dog who shared the home and Buddy felt a need to protect him too. *I need to look after us – dad doesn't do that. I don't like the smoke, and neither does Chester – it hurts us. I know we just need to wait, but it's hard.*

This was very tricky. When I fed back to his mum, Stephanie, all I said was that she had a sensible dog who took a lot on and was often confused by the changes in his dad's behaviour to him, Chester and their mum. I then asked whether she knew what he got upset about, and before I knew it she revealed many of the same details that I'd been given by Buddy. Stephanie confirmed that, when she wasn't there, Roger didn't feed the dogs, hence Buddy's comments. Additionally, he was a heavy smoker and Stephanie had already taken the dogs to the vet as they were affected by it.

I was prepared for Stephanie to end contact with me – this often happens when animals raise personal, difficult issues about their human families with me; I am, after all, a complete stranger – so I have to admit that I was absolutely delighted when she contacted me a few months later to say that she had actually left her husband and taken the dogs with her. What wise creatures we invite into our lives, and what an awful lot we sometimes put them through.

Thankfully, there are also lighter moments when animals reveal secrets, particularly when these are about their own desires. While communicating with Felix the parrot, I had barely been asking about his health for a minute when he screeched, *Sex! I want sex!* There was little room for confusion there, but he didn't stop: he wanted to make sure I had completely got it. I had this image of him flapping wildly, constantly squawking, *Sex! Sex! I want sex! Tell her to make sure I get sex!* Just as animals send me the sensations of joy or pain, Felix gave me a completely new experience of receiving a psychic orgasm – all the while he was sitting demurely on his perch. He felt like a real cheeky chappie who liked to entertain people. I felt that he really needed some sunshine around him, and that his desire for female physical attention was also linked to a more specific wish for company. This poor bird was lonely and needed a girlfriend.

Luckily, his mum saw the funny side of her obsessed bird. However, on a serious note, she was concerned about him and had already been trying to find a mate for him (these birds mate for life) but he was such a rare breed that locating a female for him was proving to be extremely difficult. All the same, she was clearly committed to keeping up her worldwide search for his life partner.

My next client was Max the corgi. Now, whether or not he had been eavesdropping into my conversation with Felix I don't know, but he had exactly the same request. Max was incredibly anxious and worried when I tuned in. He was picking up on his mum's worry and was in turn worrying for her, which was later confirmed by her. He was basically a happy dog, who like to play and interact, but his back legs were extremely tired – exhausted, in fact – and this was frustrating him.

As soon as I felt the exhaustion in his back legs I received the word *rabbit* and the phrase *like a rabbit*. When I fed back to his mum, she laughed and said, 'That's because my bitch is in heat and Max is constantly at her wanting to get some action. He's too small for her but he doesn't give up trying – hence the exhausted back legs. He'd be at it like a rabbit if he could manage!'

Just another weird day in the life of a pet whisperer.

Chapter 14

Meeting My Animal Guides

From the moment the door to animal communication opened with Dan, I felt I was on a path, a journey, and that I was being guided – but by whom? This sense of guidance continued and still continues with every animal I work with. In the early days I had been taught that we all have 'guides', so many years ago I decided to take some time to connect with my animal helpers.

One day, I sat quietly with the intent purpose of connecting with my spirit guide through meditation. The first time I did the exercise it was a rabbit who presented himself to me. The energy was light and vibrant and when the rabbit appeared there was a sense of contentment and brightness. On another occasion, when I undertook the same exercise, a bear stepped forward – a huge brown bear that seemed extremely powerful and strong. He was there to offer his strength and protection to me as I worked.

As time went on, I was also visited by a dog and cat, both of whom I felt I had known at some point of my life, and I became much more interested in finding out what I could learn from these creatures and their visits, as they all had something to offer – sometimes strength, some-times courage or love, but usually patience.

Animal energy is something that is referred to in a great deal of ancient tales and myths – stories from times when we ran in parallel to other animals, rather than viewing ourselves as superior. Ironically, as we get more and more technology in our lives, and as we become increasingly distracted from nature, many people are taking stock, looking back to the old ways of living and being, and realizing that there is no need to learn things all over again when there is knowledge already in existence.

For ancient Native Americans, the link between humans and animal energy was very clear – in fact, in most ancient civilizations there tended to be bonds between humans and animals. In the past we may have hunted or eaten animals, but we also learned from them. To this day, we carry some of this knowledge with us – for example, does your cat know when there's a storm coming, and do you believe her now, given that she's been right on so many occasions? Do you feel that winter snows aren't far away when the first robin appears in your garden, or when a sense of winter sadness comes over you when you see the geese depart? We are syn-chronized to these movements and the intelligence these animals have, even if we have allowed our own natural intelligence to lapse.

Animal spirit guides are there for all, if we open our

eyes and hearts to them. I soon found that the message from each of my guides was often the same – patience and love, patience and love. My brown bear represented physical and emotional strength, and I often felt the former was depleted when I had been using up too much of the latter, for the work I was now doing could be draining if I didn't look after myself properly. The appearance of my bear was a sign to take things easy, to slow down and make sure my batteries were charged. During meditation I have many times been given the paw of a bear as a gift, which represents the strength I need to do the work that is in store for me. Anyone who takes a walk down this path of animal communication will find that they too have animal guides to help and enlighten them.

With a willing and open heart, our animal guides can easily be invited to make an appearance in our lives. This is a process anyone can do and I would encourage you to try. There are lots of guided meditations available to help you connect with your animal guide. Many of these meditations involve travelling deep within mother earth – really connecting with the earth, absorbing and sharing and being part of the same grounding and nurturing energy. While I connect and use earth energy everyday in my daily work and life, I find this style of meditation ignites my claustrophobia, so I've had to work on developing meditative techniques that are less threatening to me, but equally as powerful in connecting with my guides. I am going to share my techniques with you, so that you too can try to access your animal spirit guide.

Find a quiet place where you are unlikely to be disturbed. As this is a special meditation, you might want to prepare your room with various embellishments, such as a lighted candle, soft music, crystals or relaxing scents. To begin with, make yourself physically comfortable, preferably with your feet connecting with the floor. Close your eyes and take in a deep cleansing breath through the nose. Release the breath through your mouth and push all the air out of your body. Take three deep breaths and, on each exhalation, imagine all your stress, anxiety and worries leaving you. Feel the tension leave your body, as you begin to relax.

Now, see a white light shining ahead in the distance. Imagine walking towards it and seeing a doorway waiting for you. Make that door something beautiful to you – is it marble, or wood, or is it covered in jewels? Is it made of liquid? What colour is it? Now step forward and open the door – there is a gorgeous, fertile forest awaiting you. There are trees, flowers, bushes, everything you want to see. Do you want a river in there? A waterfall? Have one! This is your space – a safe space – your own magical haven where you will learn how to ignite your innate ability to communicate with animals. Look around and allow yourself to become completely absorbed by your surroundings, let all of your senses come alive.

Slowly walk down the path that has appeared before you. Become aware of how it feels underfoot: is it grassy? Stony? Wooden? The path takes you to a large clearing. Stop and breathe in the wonder of this enchanting place and all it has to offer you. When you are ready, invite your animal guide to step forward and greet you. Whoever or whatever appears, accept them immediately and give thanks for them coming. Ask them what you can do that will help you communicate with animals. Your guide is there for you – listen and trust. Remember what has been said so you can be sure to act upon it later when you return to the physical world.

As you prepare to leave your guide, ask if they have a parting message or gift for you. Accept gratefully whatever the message or gift is. If you do not understand its meaning or significance, ask your guide. Assure your guide that you will use their gift in your communication work and that you will return to them again to learn all that they have to teach you.

In order to always stay connected to your guide, imagine a ball of beautiful pink light emanating from your heart and send this pink light of love direct to the heart of your guide – creating a beautiful bridge of love between you and them. Each time you communicate with an animal, invite your guide to step forward and meet you on the bridge of love that connects you so they can work with you and guide you in all your communications with animals.

Thank your guide and say goodbye in whichever way pleases you. Walk back along the path until you reach the door that brought you to this magical place. Step through the doorway and as it clicks shut bring your awareness back to your physical world. Take three deep breaths and open your eyes.

Write everything down that your guide shared with you. This ensures that you do not forget these valuable messages and lessons, but in time will also serve as a record of your own growth as you progress on your spiritual path.

Now – did you enjoy that, or do you feel relief that you did it when the house was empty? If this is completely new to you then it's perfectly understandable to be a bit unsure, or even embarrassed, by trying such techniques – but, come on, what have you got to lose? The more I do it, the more I learn. The more I learn, the more I can help. I have a number of guides but I usually only see one at a time. Different guides will come through at different times – depending on what I need or what I am meant to learn. Just be open to what they have to teach you.

What my animal guides have done for me is immeasurable. I am often hurt, upset, or uplifted by the communication I do, and my animal guides are always there to remind me to take some time out, that I must to protect and look after myself or I'm no use to anyone. Like everyone, I have 'real life' to deal with as well, and no matter how many amazing pet-whisperer sessions have gone on in my week, there's always ironing to be done, and shopping to do. I'm a mum and that is vitally important to me – there's no point in me helping others if my own children are neglected. In fact, as I write this, with a baby on the way and a wedding to organize, I can't help but hope all of my clients are going to have very straightforward issues to deal with for the next few months! However, all that said, recognizing the need for balance hasn't always been easy.

My former life (as I see it) as a community-education worker has helped hugely and I apply lessons learned in that world to this one whenever I can. This may seem odd to some people, given that my previous job meant that I was often dealing with pregnant teenagers or addicts or homeless people, all of which seem a world away from a displaced mongrel or a tetchy moggy. To me, though, it doesn't clash at all. What I learned from my training and my years in work was the importance of listening – people (and animals) don't often need an 'expert' to come in and decide what should happen. More likely, the very individuals who are feeling left out on the edges of society have been talked at for far too long by far too many; someone keeping quiet and just taking on board what they're saying is much more effective than coming in with another list of so-called solutions.

As I mentioned at the beginning of my story, when Dan first came to me one of the only ways I could process his repeated appearances was to ask myself what I would have done had a young person kept coming to me. There is no way I would have ignored them, so why would I do that with Dan? To this day, that is still the way I think – it's not my job to judge or to put my agenda on to a client's needs. I'll help where I can, but I won't force things. With this work comes frustration when I can't help. Not all animals want their guardians to be informed of what they tell me, and without my counsellor hat on I would find that unbearable. If a young person had come to me and said they were being abused or were in danger, then, of course, I would have alerted the appropriate authorities, and I would do the same for any animal; but when emotional issues are involved, I have to respect the client. If a teenager had been causing trouble, for example, and they confided in me that it was actually a way of getting their despair and depression out of their system, I would keep their confidence while exploring more positive solutions with them to help resolve their difficulties.

Similarly, if a dog reveals to me that she is heartbroken that her mum and dad are planning to move and she'll never see her friends again, I do have to check whether I can pass that information on. Sometimes they don't want me to and I have to respect their decisions and their confidentiality. Whether person or dog, the rules are the same: I have to be there for them; if I betray them and reveal their emotions, they'll never come back to me – and that would be worse, for they may be left with no one to confide in or, even worse, no trust left to confide in anyone.

Considering all of this, I soon realized that I needed to learn to protect myself – and my animal guides helped enormously in doing so. The white light that I see in my visualization to meet my guides is something I wrap myself in before I start work. This acts as a protective barrier – allowing energy and communication to travel freely between me and the animal, but preventing anything negative or harmful penetrating the protective shield of pure white light around me.

I had such a headache when I first communicated with Dan, and that warned me that I have a sensitivity to taking on my clients' pain. As soon as I'm finished communicating, I disconnect from the animal and cleanse myself with a beautiful shower of pure white light, and I completely indulge myself in it! Hanging onto animals' guilt, pain or fear helps no one. If you are working properly and effectively that shouldn't happen. Protect yourself first, then when you disconnect, it's finished – keeping both you and the animal you are working with safe and protected.

Chapter 15

Trying to Explain

As my life was becoming more and more centred around animal-communication work, the people around me had a lot of questions. My children and family were all really supportive – even if they didn't quite 'get' what was going on – but friends in particular often asked the most obvious questions that put into perspective what I was actually doing. How does it work? What happens? Do you hear what animals are thinking when you walk past them on the street?

Sometimes it's only when people ask that I think about it, but there are certain things I do and experience that will enlighten anyone reading this book and will also, hopefully, aid them in trying to communicate as well. As I said in the earlier chapter, since the beginning of time all civilizations have recognized the power and wisdom of animals, but, for psychic communication to work, we must also recognize the power and wisdom within *ourselves*. With an open mind and open heart, you may very well find your life changed – and wonder how you managed without this knowledge.

When I ask an animal a question, I receive from them pictures, feelings, words, thoughts and emotions. For example, were I to ask a horse what part of his body was sore, I might feel pain in an area of my body that corresponds to his: my wrists equate to a fetlock, knees to hocks, hands and feet to hooves, and so on. The horse may also send me a picture of the area or send me a picture of him moving to show me where he is lame. Sometimes the animal will even show or tell me how the injury happened. I act as the translator and the voice for the animal. I take all of this information and put it into words for the guardian to understand.

There are four main methods of communication and I use them all in my work as a pet whisperer. We already possess all of these skills – they just need to be honed for communication work to be effective. With clairsentience (clear feeling), I can send and receive emotions and feelings. It is different to claircognisance (clear knowing), which is a sense of simply *knowing* something – knowing that things are right or wrong, accurate or false.

I have seen some female animals, just like their human counterparts, who have a preference for certain types of food when pregnant – now, we all know that there are usually real physiological reasons for cravings in human mums-to-be, so why would animals not also have that knowledge, given that they are so much closer to nature than we are? They *just know* what they need – and I just know that they know. Similarly, an ill or troubled creature will often be able to tell me what he or she wants access to in their diets. For domestic pets, that can be hard; horses sometimes have more freedom. However, what I do accept is that they're right – and I actually get a physical sense of that when I communicate with them.

The hardest part of recognizing that claircognisance is actually a trustworthy option has been, for me, to simply go with it. It took me a long time to trust the information and to stop questioning myself – even ridiculing myself. But the information was always right and I no longer question. I've had a sensible life, so to simply accept that something is right without knowing 'why' or 'how' has been hard. I worked with one greyhound who sent tremendous feelings of grief and abandonment. I just knew, without asking, that this was related to her having 'no mother'. Now, clearly she couldn't have no mother at all, so had she passed over or had there been a lack of attachment or early separation? It almost doesn't matter, because the emotion is the same whether there has actually been a death or not: it's still grief and loss. This poor dog hadn't moved on, and the depth of loss was so huge and deep that I was certain there had been a death. It turned out that she had been part of a greyhound-farming ring and that she had indeed been dragged away from her mother before she was weaned, a fact that was affecting her soul so much that she couldn't stop grieving – I just knew this was the case.

Clairaudience (clear hearing) is the psychic ability to hear things – voices or sounds or words. When Dan first appeared to me, I heard things very quickly. I tend not to have a spoken-out-loud conversation with clients, but there are words passed between us psychically – or in my head. That sounds crazy, doesn't it? But the fact is that our heads are incredibly powerful places, with huge amounts of energy, and it actually seems quite reasonable when you think of it to pass that energy between one individual and another. With Dan, the words I heard were full of character. When he said 'Hiya!' to me, it was a very bouncy, very youthful sort of greeting. I usually hear things in my own voice, but with different words or intonations to the ones I would use. At other times, there is a totally different sounding voice in there – with Barney, every word was laden with patience.

I believe that clairaudience involves not simply listening to the words, but listening to the meaning of a conversation too. What an animal doesn't say is as important as what they do say. Barney gave me a lot of information but kept away from agreeing to a body scan until I asked him again and offered my reassurances. A cat I worked with called Fifi was very evasive whenever I asked her about her scratching. I found out that she was worried about her mum, and actually discovered that Fifi needed her mum to work on herself – then the scratching would stop.

When I dealt with a Dutch dog called Oskar, he spoke to me in English. Psychic communication is not bound by the earthly limitations of a specific language. The animal gives you information in whatever format will best allow you to make sense of it and that is why information comes to you in your native tongue. This is why they often send words that have no meaning in the animal world, but which are shorthand for us. So, I will have animals talk about husbands or wives – clearly, they don't marry, but they know that these are phrases which human communicators apply and they help us as much as they can.

They can also use clairaudience to 'interrupt' my thoughts. I was once waiting for a client who wanted to meet in advance of setting up an animal-communication session for her dog. As I sat there he piped up with, *You'll be waiting a while – my mum's always late.* When she eventually arrived and I told her this, she was shocked but agreed that she never, ever got anywhere in time. She certainly didn't have any doubts about setting up a session after that! As with Dan, I often get reactions such as *Duh!* if I've taken my time to make sense of things and the animal is getting impatient with me, or if it was something simple – this comes through as clear as day.

Clairvoyance (clear seeing) is probably the mode of communication that most people are familiar with – even if they are thinking of spooky, haunted happenings. In my world and life, the stripped-down definition of the word is most appropriate. It simply refers to seeing pictures in my mind. These pictures can be happy or sad, comforting or threatening, they can also be about the past or the future. Many animals will send information in picture form. Sometimes they use pictures to show me something I recognize from my own life, which I can apply to what they are trying to tell me – I might not know their house or their location or their family, so they will show me my own. I often get animals sending me images of children to symbolise pups – after all, the relationship is the same! Clairvoyance is very useful when doing tracking work (locating a lost animal). If I'm tracking an animal, then I will ask them to show me road signs or landmarks, which may help me locate them. This ability to see things via pictures can be used for anything, such as where they sleep, live, play, what their toys are like, the other animals they share a home with, what favourite foods they enjoy and so forth.

So, in summary: clairsentience is the ability to send and receive emotion to and from your animal friends; clairaudience is the ability to hear telepathic information in whatever language you speak; clairvoyance is the ability to see via pictures, sometimes a moving image like a video clip; and claircognisance is the ability to 'just know' or intuit information. When discussing an animal's ill health I will often just know that it's the stomach or liver causing problems because of the way that the energy pulls me there at a million miles per hour (but I always have to remind guardians that I am not a vet nor a substitute for visiting a vet).

With animal work, when talking to the human carer, I usually get a shiver that runs from the top of my head down to the bottom of my feet when I've 'hit the button' and uncovered the core issue. I will say something when giving feedback that I had not thought about until I started, with no consideration of the words or language that I was going to use – it just comes out. I'll think, *Why did I say that? Where did that come from?* because I may even use words or a phrase that I never normally use, only to find that it is the one thing that exposes the underlying issue.

I once asked the mum of a troubled donkey, 'Do you have shame issues?' I would never ordinarily put something as bluntly as that and was actually horrified by myself. Completely mortified, I put my hand to my mouth as if trying to pull the words back in – it felt as though my mouth had a mind of its own – just as the poor woman burst out crying. She did have deeply buried shame issues and had needed to hear those exact words to feel 'permission' to talk about her problems, which the donkey was mirroring.

There are other ways of describing these communication tools that are used by other communicators and that you may have come across. Moving video is self-explanatory and is when pictorial information is received like a movie. As previously stated, this is most helpful in tracking work, when I can be shown a route an animal has taken.

I was once sent an image by a tabby called Betty who told me that she had gone *down the path, took a right turn, where I was chased by a dog into an open field with a wood at the side.* I followed her along this route before she switched to clairvoyance to indicate a tree with something red on it. I knew that it wasn't a flower, but I wasn't sure exactly what was being indicated. I sent the feedback to Betty's mum who confirmed the location when she found her – sadly, it was too late and a fox had got to the poor kitty, but the tree had a piece of red plastic caught in the branches.

Cats sometimes share their hunting territory in this way too; they like to show off! Often animals will show how they have sustained injuries by using this medium – at times it's like watching a DVD.

Amelia Kinkade employs useful terms of her own for some of the communication tools. The first is X-ray vision, sometimes referred to as 'medical gestalt' or 'body scan'. As previously referred to, body scanning is the ability of the human communicator to use their own body as an instrument to determine if and when the animal is in pain. With Barney I could utilize this to identify his arthritis and leg pain. With a horse called Blackjack I needed to determine whether his jaw was broken – I could tell from how the bone felt that it wasn't and this matched the hunch of both his mum and vet too.

There have been lots of cases whereby human carers have phoned me about their animals and I have intuitively or energetically picked up that it is the front right leg or the back left leg or the right side of the stomach that needs to be attended to, and they are often amazed. To me, it's just energy, and I pick up where it stops flowing, because my training in energy therapy has heightened my energy sensitivity.

The other term that Amelia has developed is the beautifully named 'starlight vision', which is a form of mediumship. This is the ability to send and receive messages from beloved animal friends on the other side of the rainbow bridge. I used to think this was something special or mystical and out of my reach, but, as the cases illustrated in this book have shown, it really is no different to connecting and communicating with an animal here on earth. It's all energy and I'm merely connecting with the soul of the animal, which lives on after death.

All of these descriptions are simply ways of categorizing what is often difficult to explain. People may ask 'How do you do it and why do you do it?' For me, the real question is: why would we *not* want to talk to animals?

Chapter 16

Jack's Story

The ways in which I was able to send and receive information were developing every day and, a few years after I had first met Dan, I had accepted that this was my calling. I felt blessed to be doing this work that had been brought to me by the animals themselves, and there were some clients who seemed to have so many issues wrapped up in one body that I was still blown away by what could happen.

So it was with Jack.

Joanne asked me to communicate with her one-year-old Hamiltonstovare puppy, Jack. She was really worried about him after the loss of his brother, Ben, from the same litter. Joanne wasn't certain of the exact circumstances of Ben's death, and knew only that he had been shot by a farmer.

When I first tuned in, Jack was terribly depressed and non-communicative – the most non-communicative animal I'd ever come across. He was presenting as lethargic and uninterested in anything. He didn't want to talk about his brother but was suffering from keeping it all inside. This was a dog who was getting by on his own;

he was almost forcing his own self-sufficiency and independence, even though there was a lot of need in him. He wanted reassurance and love, but he was pining for his brother very much. His way of dealing with it was, understandably, to mourn, but also to act as if he didn't need anyone.

He didn't want to talk about Ben so I concentrated on non-threatening things to build up our communication. He showed me plenty of green space and I felt that he liked where he lived very much. When I asked him where he slept, he did what many animals do, which was to show me an image that was familiar to me. The one he sent was a lovely one of my grandparents' old house, which had a Rayburn in the kitchen. This was a family room and their dogs (of which I was terrified) all slept there. He sent me this image again at a later session, and I deduced that Jack liked to sleep in the kitchen or family area.

I asked him whether he wanted me to do some therapy work on him and there was an element of defiance in his response. He didn't answer me and refused to agree or disagree with me going forward. When an animal hasn't explicitly said that they don't want me to do work on them, I use my own judgement to decide whether or not to progress; in this case I determined that Jack needed work on his grief and security issues. Surprisingly, as soon as I began, I was immediately flooded with huge waves of enjoyment and peace.

I felt that Jack was lying around more than usual but

was lethargic in nature. He did inform me that he was not sleeping particularly well, hence the lounging about. He was missing his brother dreadfully and scored his mood at two out of ten. I received sensations that, while he and Ben hadn't necessarily played together all the time, there was a feeling of closeness; this sense was accompanied by the words, *He was just there*. I also felt that his brother was most definitely the boss in their relationship.

In our next session Jack was still very low, but he was willing to send me more images, rather than lots of words, which I managed to piece together. Both pups had run off to play hunt, which they often did. Ben had gone into a field of sheep and had begun to worry them. He had actually bitten one of the sheep so was shot by the farmer. After Ben's death Jack became distant and lethargic, and never really recovered, hence his mum's call to me. I felt that Jack understood what had happened to his brother and why, but he didn't seem able to move on: when I asked if he would like a new companion, he sent me an image of two hounds together but my sense was that this was his brother – meaning that, at the moment, he wanted only Ben, no one else.

As Jack and Ben were hunting dogs, it had been usual for them to go off and not come back when called. This had been a huge challenge for Joanne, so I suggested that she stimulate Jack's natural abilities in a safe and controlled environment. I had to send Jack horrible pictures of what would happen to him if he ran off into the farmer's fields and worried the sheep. Because of the difficulty of extracting information from Jack during both this session and the last one, I asked if he felt able to express his emotions, particularly his grief, over the loss of his brother. He sent me the image of him and a young girl – there was great affection towards him from her. She felt like the youngest child in the house, and it was very apparent that she too shared his sadness and therefore understood his pain. I also felt that she was quite sensitive to Jack's grief and he was picking up on her sadness (our animals have an incredible way of picking up on and carrying our pain, both physical and emotional).

With time and therapy work, Jack began tentatively intimating that he was more open to a new dog companion. Circumstances created an opportunity for Joanne to re-home another dog and, whilst we all shared concerns that it still might be a little too soon, the bull was taken by the horns and Flea was duly introduced to the household. When I first tuned into him after Flea had been brought home, I was delighted that he sent me sensations of bounciness – perhaps he has been won over, I thought. On sifting through, however, it became clear that he was showing me how he used to be, in comparison to how he feels now. The lethargy was still there. Again, I felt the same defensiveness that had appeared in the first session, so reverted once more to small talk. However, this clever dog knew what I was up to – *I'm not the only one who needs to get some things sorted out*, he said. *You need to be a bit better at answering the phone during your work hours.* This blew me away. He was absolutely right – I was so often in a rush that I just said 'hello' instead of a more welcoming reception for clients. What sound advice; but I knew he was just trying to distract me from dealing with his problems. There was little I could do with him that day. He was not happy with Flea's arrival, and had gone into himself and was not ready to communicate at all, so I sent him healing and closed off.

At the next session, Jack was happy for the first time. He sent me sensations of him exploring, finding new things with his head nuzzling and pushing. *How do you rate your mood?* I asked. He told me it was eight out of ten, the first time it had ever been above two or three. There was a lot of bounciness and tail wagging going on, at the same time as he sent me a video. There was an open gate with a track or path on the left of a field. It felt as if the ground was rising as we went up the track. There was a house at the top of the rise and I had the distinct sensation of rooting. I heard a voice calling Jack; however, despite being able to hear this voice, the rooting was much more important to him. The rooting was Jack's job. Jack would come home when his work was finished. I felt a distinct opening of his heart with this video, a real expansion of freedom and light. As I could hear Jack being called, I asked him if he had permission to go on his hunt. *Er, no,* he said sheepishly. *But I really had fun.* Apparently he'd had a small search team looking for him for more than two hours! Usually I ask if there is anything the animal would like me to pass on to his family, but before I could finish this question Jack came in with: *Can you say thank you to my mum and tell her that I love her?*

Joanne had asked me to check with Jack whether he would enjoy dog-training classes. *That's a good idea,* he said, then became very thoughtful. *I need to knuckle down, don't I?* He knew himself that this would be good for him, that stimulation and new challenges were just what he needed to move on from his grief and loss. I also sensed that he took advantage of Joanne a lot and pushed the boundaries; therefore we had a discussion about consequences. Jack felt that he had been scolded here but admitted that he knew about consequences. I immediately felt a rush of exuberance – very puppylike. That's when I remembered that he was still a puppy, despite all that he had been through at far too early an age. *How can we reach a compromise, Jack? Do you have any suggestions? Is there somewhere you can root around and be exuberant where it's safe?* He immediately sent me an image of some woods and the message that he would *work hard for mum.* As the woods were a fun place for Jack to be but not a safe place, Joanne was encouraged to stimulate Jack's need to hunt by hiding his food and toys in the garden and nearby fields, where he could follow scent trails but in a completely safe environment. Jack took some convincing but showing him the consequences worked.

We then moved on to how he felt about having a companion. His response was favourable, but he wasn't ready just yet. I also felt that he needed someone he could take charge of and that this might be an older dog. Interestingly, he sent me an image of a puppy. I felt that he needed another dog who would keep him in check, too, and that none of this related to Flea. He was open to someone, but not that particular dog.

At the next session, I immediately on connection with Jack felt light, lifted and happy – a real tangible buoyancy. It felt as if he had been waiting for me and was pleased to see me. I also sensed excitement and change in the air – and as though Flea was no longer around. I felt frustration, and the feeling of being housebound, as if he was not getting out enough, although I knew that Joanne took him out a lot. Could this be symbolic of not being able to remove himself from the other dog, I wondered? *Can you tell me about the other dog?* I asked. Jack sent me a photograph in which Flea was being pushed out of the picture – it felt as if Jack was actively doing that. This imagery was immediately followed by a sense of isolation, which was not negative. I had absolutely no doubt that Jack was clearly stating that he did not want Flea around. He also sent me a combination of imagery and feelings of Flea being an excitable, happy dog, a real entertainer. It felt that Jack was on the sidelines watching and felt isolated from his family, which was – naturally – contributing to his low mood.

I had sensed at the beginning that Jack's happiness was because of Flea not being around, but it felt like Jack's low mood was in the present and not the past. *Is Flea still living with you?* I asked. I got *Yes*, immediately followed by *No*. We went around in circles a little, but my interpretation of the conflicting information was that, yes, Flea was still around, but Jack knew that the other dog was leaving, hence the excitement and change in the air. Jack knew that Joanne had realized Flea had to go. Immediately on receiving this information there was an increase in energy and mood. *Can you tell my mum something?* he asked. *Can you tell her that I appreciate that she's trying – and thank her?* He and his mum are working much better together now with their alternative hunting and he even has a new playmate he's happy with.

Jack took a huge amount of work and time, but I feel his case is vitally important in demonstrating the many ways in which animals can use different communication methods, as well as highlighting how huge my journey had been in order to be able to interpret this mass of material and come to some coherent conclusion. Clairsentience, clairvoyance, clairaudience and claircognisance were all utilized here, as were moving video and X-ray vision. Although he was still a puppy, Jack was actually a very clever dog to be able to use every available option to make me understand what had happened to him and what was continuing to go on in his life. Whether Jack realized it or not, him showing me my grandparents' Rayburn made me look at my childhood and created space for me to reflect greatly on just how far I had come.

Sometimes I find the journey I've been on so incredible that I can hardly make sense of it myself. Putting pen to paper and trying to get some shape of it for other people has been a revelation, because this, too, has shown me that there has been a plan to my life that, while I may not have been aware of it, has been moving me towards this point all of my days. I had a fairly ordinary upbringing and, as I have mentioned, wasn't pulled towards animals; in fact, I was actively scared of dogs, – terrified, even. Jack sending me that image of my grandparents' kitchen took me back to how I used to be, which was exactly what he wanted, I'm sure.

My Grandpa and Grandma had a sheep farm, and whilst I loved them both very much and enjoyed being with them in the peace and tranquility of the countryside, I was scared of the sheep and terrified of the sheepdogs. I never touched them and would even cry if the house-dogs came near me. It was years before I would go downstairs in the morning if there was no one there and the pets were running around. There was a waterfall that I loved on the farm, but my sister Samantha and I had to cross a field of sheep to get to it. She'd be fine but I always thought they'd attack me so I'd walk around the perimeter, by the fence, even though it was much longer. Some days I wouldn't even be willing to do that, no matter how much Samantha laughed at me. I'd watch her confidently stride across the field and wonder how she did it – how could she not be petrified? To me, the dogs, the sheep and the cattle were threatening creatures, always suggesting the possibility of attack, and I actively avoided going near them.

I could have had access to animals if I'd wanted it but I consciously stayed away from them. My mum had grown up on this farm too but she was never an animal person either; she'd never harm them or see one harmed – she just didn't get them, just like me. As I said, Jack's images reminded me of how far I had come. I was a very analytical person during the early and adult years of my life before Dan appeared, very left-brained, and I've had to learn on this amazing journey to just go with some things and to go back to my roots and re-identify with who I am and what's important to me. That took a . while. It was difficult and painful. I believe that to get to the person you are meant to be is often a tricky journey. We all need to uncover our own demons and work with them until we can be at ease. I didn't just decide one day that I was going to be an animal psychic. I was happy, I enjoyed my work, but the question was whether I was happy *enough*. Was I truly content? No. I knew at times that I was lacking that deep spiritual feeling, of living the life that I was meant to live and for which I am now grateful every day. To some people this may sound rather woolly, but why would you not want to have the best life you could possibly have, full of wonderful experiences and different every day? I'm lucky, but so many other people could be too if they would only open themselves up to the wonderful possibilities that are out there.

Chapter 17

What Animals Know

Many people ask me whether I have any religious convictions and the extent to which such matters affect my work with animals. To be honest, I have none that would fit in with any straightforward church on the high street, but I do have beliefs – how could I not, given what has happened to me?

I was raised as a Protestant Christian and attended church weekly as well as going to Bible class and Girls' Brigade. When I was about eighteen, I had turned my back on religion (much to the upset of my mum) when I went out into the world. My journey of discovery brought me to complementary therapy and I also discovered angels. I attended a few workshops and really enjoyed connecting with the beautiful angelic energy I learned about. I know there are many people who will be shaking their heads at this point and saying they don't believe in such nonsense, but I'd like you to bear in mind that I was – and still am in many ways – a very practical, pragmatic person. I was working in an area of employment that showed me some of the awful directions people's lives could take. It doesn't matter whether you think those who use drugs are weak or misguided, whether they succumb to peer pressure or are selfish; no one can surely deny the terrible effects that ensue. I was dealing with those effects every single day of my working life. I wasn't living in some perfect little world where I wafted around thinking of angels to fill my hours, but I saw the incredible benefits that both complementary therapy and a belief in things that often can't be explained really can have on people who have all but given up.

I began to question the whole notion of God and angels and how, in my head, the two went together. I had, after all, been taught as a child that the angels carried out God's work, so it was perhaps not such a big step to believe that they too could be accessed in much the same way that many people have no trouble believing that God can be called upon in times of need. As my learning (and experience) flourished, I became less focused on whether it was God or the angels or indeed any other being at work. All I knew was that there was an almighty force in our world – a universal force. And that once this energy was tapped into, and we were consciously connected with it, it became incredibly powerful – powerful enough to connect us with each other, powerful enough to create change and powerful enough to heal.

My belief now is that there is something out there; whether you call it God, Shiva, angels, spirit or Allah doesn't matter to me. I don't get hung up on the names, because for me it is all the same. There is a force greater than us that connects us to each other. We are all made of energy and live in a world with an energetic force field that has been scientifically proven by people much more clever than me. With patience and practice we can connect with this powerful energy and communicate with each other on an energetic level, whether in this lifetime or another. So, yes, I believe there is most definitely continuity within life – I see it every day in the work I do now. We are all connected and unconsciously connecting all the time; we are often just too busy to take the time to notice.

It can take people by surprise when any of this actually makes an impact in their lives. One guy I was working with when I was in the Drugs Project, a long-term heroin user who was trying to come off drugs, came to a complementary therapy session I'd organized and said that he didn't believe a word of it. It was all 'hokey pokey', in his words, but he trusted me as his worker so he'd give it a go. When he came out afterwards, he was walking as if he was on something. 'I swear I've taken nothing,' he said, 'but I have never felt this relaxed when I'm clean before. I can't believe it!' That was an eye opener for me and really showed me the power of complementary therapies – because of the experiences of clients who had difficult and stressful lives and didn't believe anything could help. I still receive revelations every day and I honestly believe that my previous work is not a million miles away from what I do now – grief and loss, hurt and anger, pain and suffering are common to all species. Animals know that even better than we do.

There are times – many times – when the messages I receive from an animal are as much about their guardian as they are about the animal itself. This can be a difficult area to deal with. Not everyone is open to being told things about themselves, their character or their relationships if they have initially asked you to help with their pet. However, I have also found that most people are incredibly receptive to the messages I feel it is my duty to pass on. Perhaps they wouldn't be quite so open if they came from another human being directly, but the fact that they love and care for their animal enough to ask me to be involved in the first place suggests that there is an emotional attachment which allows them to recognize what is being passed to them through me.

This was certainly the case when I was asked to work with a beautiful horse called Tasha. Her mum, Celia, had contacted me to see what I could pick up about her from a photographic reading. As is generally the case, I didn't ask for any more information, as I prefer to go in 'cold' and let the animal lead the communication session. With a reading such as that with Tasha, I wanted to leave things open and allow her to talk about what was on her mind.

As soon as I tuned into the photograph, I was flooded with feelings and information not about her, but about Celia, her mum. She told me instantly that her mum was nervous and worried about her. I could tell from this that

Tasha was a loving and affectionate horse, as her main priority was Celia, but there were some other issues that she was not going to be upfront about immediately. There was definitely a sense of her holding back and that is often the case when the animal wants to talk about their mum or dad rather than themselves. So I allowed her to chat about Celia as much as she wanted, which allowed me to deduce that Celia was having confidence issues. But it felt deeper than Tasha was voicing. There were confidence issues with both of them. Tasha knew that she was loved – *I know it, I feel it, I like it because I want it* – but, despite this, I sensed strong emotional needs around her, needs which I thought were being met, especially the desire to be loved and feel extra special. As we worked together to unpack the information and make sense of it all. I realized that I may have made assumptions when I thought this aspect related to Tasha, and wondered whether it was actually linked to Celia herself.

I felt there was some sadness in Tasha's background and later on in the session she sent me imagery and sensations of loss. This led me to believe that she had given birth to two foals at some point and still missed them terribly. Celia had only recently acquired Tasha and didn't actually know if this was the case, but a vet confirmed that she still had remnants of milk in her teats.

She was a beautiful girl and sent me an image of her tail in plaits – I got the impression that this was what she wanted rather than something that was done for her at the moment, and she also wanted to emphasize that she was a dainty young lady, sending me the number *17* with this point. I later found out that she was just slightly under seventeen hands in height. Tasha was a lovely character. Although she was easy to engage in conversation, she dominated and led it, therefore continually avoiding any difficult questions I might want to put to her. She was a little defensive and not too willing, at that early stage, to delve deeply into anything. This was further confirmed near the end of the session when she closed up upon my asking about her stable, so I made a note to follow that up next time. I felt that she had so much more to tell but something also made me feel that it would all be very much on her own terms.

At the next session, all of this was confirmed. Tasha could be an easy horse to work with but I also felt there would need to be a degree of work on Celia's part to get to that place with her. Once she was there, there would be a wonderful relationship of mutual respect and love. Moving towards such a spiritual connection would take time and patience but it would be worth it.

A lot of information came through, all of which Celia told me was accurate, but I was intrigued by how much of it was about her. *Tell her I'm not Emma, tell her to stop comparing me to Emma.* Celia did say that her previous horse was indeed called Emma, and that she would try to stop comparing them. Tasha was still setting the agenda in this session and I realized that she would be making me work just as hard as she was telling me Celia would be working too.

The following day, she was upfront about matters.

Mum needs to get herself sorted out.

Animals say this sort of thing more than we would perhaps like them to. They see our prevarications, our insecurities, the ways in which we don't make the best of ourselves, and they get terribly frustrated. *Did you hear me?* she asked. *Mum needs to get herself sorted out.* I told her that I had indeed heard her and that I would pass on any messages she had for Celia. *She has blocks.* I asked what sort of blocks. *She wants to be loved but she has issues – she's nervous about so many things and when she rides me she passes that nervousness on to me. I'm not nervous! She needs to stop making me that way! She needs to deal with it!* This was very interesting – Tasha was using her evolved awareness to a spectacular level and could see how Celia's problems were imprinting on their relationship. *We need to ride out together more – this will stop her being nervous. She has nothing to be nervous about from me, but she does need to get everything else sorted out. I'll take it slow; she'll be fine with me.*

Tasha was a strong horse, physically and emotionally, but her role was to be a teacher for Celia (as animals so often are) and to move her to a place of strength as well. Celia told Tasha everything, all of her hopes and fears, and Tasha knew that her mum had to change to get the most out of her life.

I very much felt that Tasha was here to fulfil a purpose with her mum. I knew her role was to move Celia forward. To metaphorically push Celia towards what she was capable of. *Mum is more comfortable with animals than with people – she prefers them – she needs to deal with that. She needs to move past issues from her own history. Her heart is closed to people. I will support her, you know – I will bear her tears.*

Those last words were so beautiful – she loved Celia so much and was delighted to be with her, but she was going to use that love to do what she could for her mum, even if it would be hard.

Tell her I love her and thank her for choosing me. Tell her to have patience with me, as it's all for a reason. Tell her to stop comparing. She doesn't just do it with me and Emma – she does it with people too. Tell her to live in the now and that it's OK to cry.

This was such a wise horse. As she mentioned it was OK for her mum to cry, I felt very strongly a connection to Celia and that she had tears locked away that needed to be shed. *Keep smiling – she has a beautiful smile,* said Tasha, *and tell her that we can ride off the pain together; we'll blow everything away.*

This was all amazing stuff. I had no idea what experiences Celia had been through – and I didn't need to know. But what I did know was that Tasha's awareness had actually afforded me the opportunity to see the world from both Celia and Tasha's perspectives. Without knowing the details, I knew I needed to be sensitive.

I had to tell Celia that she must work on her own confidence and deal with her past issues. There was a very strong link with these issues having created a closing down of her heart, which needed to be reopened. I also felt that, whilst her heart may be more closed than was helpful to her, she willingly gave to animals. This just needed to be activated with people. None of this was critical of Celia and didn't mean that she wasn't a warm person. In fact, I'd always found her to be lovely and was quite surprised by what Tasha told me. The messages were given with pure love and were received by me with no judgement – it was just part of the journey.

Celia's response was astonishing. She accepted it all and admitted that these were all issues about which she had told no one – no one but Tasha. She couldn't believe how her horse had managed to pinpoint so accurately things that had held her back for years and she was now more than willing to do this amazing animal justice by taking some therapy on board and working on herself. I was surprised too. Animals had shown themselves to be wonderful at spotting issues with their mums and dads in previous cases I'd worked on, but this was incredible. If we could all access the wisdom and love of other creatures, what a world it would be.

Chapter 18

Speaking the Same Language

A couple of years ago I went on holiday to Australia. I started off the trip by going to a fauna park on my first day. The wildlife and flowers were incredible, with colours and a vividness that I'd never seen before. It's hard to break habits, so, when I went in and saw all the animals running around, I thought I'd see if I could tune in to any of them. There were lots of wallabies in particular and one of them came through in seconds. He was incredibly grumpy. *Are you OK?* I asked him. In no uncertain terms, he told me where to go. I looked back at him as I was walking away and he met my eyes. *Go on,* he said, swearing at me again. *You and everyone else. All these young pups running around and bothering me. Bloody nuisance, everyone.* I got the message loud and clear that time from a straight-talking Australian.

After lunch, there was a tour around the park. All of the tourists were taken to see the wallabies and dingoes. One dingo was called Duncan – he was a beautiful creature, lying on a rock – and we were told about dingoes in general before their keeper, John, said he would bring out two of their newest additions. He brought out a really boisterous pup and I felt the energy as soon as he appeared; it was like he was saying, *Hiya, hiya!* This little one was very excitable and wanted to be right in there, desperate to know what everyone was doing – however, it wouldn't have taken an animal communicator to work that out, as he was young and always surrounded by people in a safe environment. So I felt he was inquisitive and needed to know what was going on and that if he didn't know he'd make it his business to find out.

John took the first pup away and came back with another one, who I immediately felt was really fearful, anxious and didn't want anyone to be there. Again, it wouldn't take an animal communicator to work that one out, as she just sat at the side of him, and John eventually did say that she was a bit more nervous than the others. I picked up so much fear from that little one.

We continued round the park and saw some stuff that, to be honest, I wasn't that interested in, such as tropical fish and birds. I then went to see the lizards. There was one who was apparently a gauld monitor, so it said on her plaque, called Claudette. She was lying on the rock, as you'd expect, but the thought that she wasn't well and off her food came into my head in a flash. She felt tired and then I got the phrase *under the weather* really clearly. *I'm off my food*, she told me wearily and I knew her tummy didn't feel good.

The guy looking after her, Billy, said that she liked mice. He got a dead one and threw it into the enclosure, and the lizard didn't move. I wasn't surprised; she'd already told me she had no appetite. Billy said that she would normally have that gobbled up but that she had been 'off her food' for a couple of days. He moved on but I stayed at the enclosure to do some more communication work. At that stage of my journey I still found live work more stressful than working with photos, but knew I was being given opportunities to practise building my confidence at live readings so wanted to grasp the opportunities as well as see what was going on with this sickly lizard.

Over and over again Claudette kept telling me she was *under the weather* and *really cold*. I asked whether there was anything that would make her feel better, and I got an image of a milky substance that I didn't recognize. What was I to do? How could I bring this up with the ranger and tell him that his lizard had been communicating with me? He'd think I was a total crackpot. I'm faced with the same scenario often and, as always, I put my own feelings aside and advocate on behalf of the unheard.

Once the tour had finished, I went to the office where I asked a young lad whether Billy was available because I wanted to have a word. He said Billy was busy but I pressed it, saying that I would really like to see him before I left. 'Well, what's it about?' he asked. Deep breath time for me. All I could say was that I worked with animals and that I was picking up that Claudette the lizard from round the back of the dingo enclosure wasn't very well. I imagine I looked like a blubbering idiot.

'Billy already knows that,' the young man said.

OK. I'd have to try a bit harder.

'Well, back home, I do animal communication.' I saw no response on his face. 'I know it's not everybody's cup of tea but I've also been chatting to one of the wallabies, the old grumpy one that doesn't like the young ones running around? I've been getting quite a lot from your animals.'

He sat up at that. 'You're right. He is a bit of a grump and he doesn't like all the nonsense the pups get up to. The young ones get boisterous and he likes peace and quiet.'

I think he then thought there might be something in this, because he told me that Billy was actually his dad and the owner of the park.

'Can you just let him know? I'll pop back later.'

As I went towards the gate, Billy shouted on me. 'Hey – hold on,' he called. 'My son says you were looking for me?' I nodded. 'He also told me some of the things you said.'

I never know how anyone is going to take my comments or interpret what I do, so I just said again that I knew it wasn't something everyone was comfortable with. 'Not everyone gets it,' I told him, 'but I'm really worried about that lizard and that's why I took the plunge to say what I did to your son.'

'Actually,' Billy interrupted, 'I think it's brilliant – absolutely fascinating. Will you come with me to see Claudette?'

I was delighted by his response and readily agreed.

She repeated to me over and over again that she was *cold, so cold,* her tummy felt poorly and she was under the weather. I knew nothing about lizards and thought that Australia would have been perfect for them, but Billy told me that it was going into winter in that part of the country. Lizards get their energy from the sun and, because the sun wasn't so strong, Claudette's energy was dipping. She didn't have the same levels of energy, she was cold, off her food – everything that I knew. I mentioned the milky substance, even though I didn't know what it was, but Billy knew and he said he'd get it for her.

His attitude was that animal communication was great – what a breath of fresh air that was. I told him the dingoes were a hoot and that the first one I'd seen was mischievous but the second one felt quite fearful. Billy said she was indeed nervous but, to me, she felt scared. He said, 'Could you please do me a favour and come back and have a look at the dingo enclosures with me?' I said I'd be delighted, how wonderful! It was a real treat. Billy took me right in beside them, giving me access that was an absolute privilege for an outsider like me. I was a little bit scared to begin with, not of the pups but of the full-size dogs. The big ones, the adults, did look a bit intimidating in their enclosure, I have to say.

I went to see the pups first. The friendly one, Ted, was out first: *Hiya, hiya!*

Immediately connecting into Ted's vivacious and

cheeky character, I said, 'Well, if you don't give that inquisitive one something to do he will create his own mischief. He's always got to be on the go, hasn't he?'

'Bloody hell, you've got that right!' he told me. 'He *is* always on the go. I've just spent thousands of dollars having to redo the water system as he'd dug it up and damaged it all. Come and have a look at this.' He took me round to the back of the enclosure and what a mess! Ted had just destroyed everything. I tuned in to the friendly pup, as he seemed to have something to tell me and was trying to break through. I couldn't stop smiling at this animal. *Hiya, hiya!* I said 'Hello' back to him and sent him lots of love; he was irresistible. I then asked him if he had anything he wanted to say. *It's not just me,* he said. I asked what he meant and he hesitated a little. I got the sense that he was wanting to talk but was protecting someone. *My sister does it too – Rosie's naughty as well. She doesn't start it, but she does join in. I am naughty, aren't I?* I told him that he was very playful but that he needed to play with his toys rather than things that could break and cause trouble, then reported back to Billy.

'Yep, you're right again – Ted starts it and she joins in, always following suit. She never instigates the mischief, but the pair of them together can really do some damage.' I told him that he really needed to find him something constructive to do or he would find even worse ways to destroy the place when they grew stronger.

Billy was worried about the female pup, Rosie – not about the fact that she was easily led, but about the fact that she was so scared. I was getting the word *feral* in my head and passed it on. He said she was from feral stock, but I didn't really know what this meant – I'd never heard the term before. Billy said that they stay wild, they have that wild element, and what worried him was that she'd be like her mum, Ruby, who had never really settled happily. I said that I'd picked up on the nervousness but she was also sending me a strong survival instinct that was telling her to stay away from people. That was exactly what Billy was worried about. 'Can you help?' he asked. 'Is there any work you can do to settle her?' I communicated with Rosie, reassured her that she had a home there for life and that the people there were committed to looking after her and helping her. I emphasized that she was surrounded by security and that no one could harm her. I felt that she was taking all this in.

I then went to see the others. Duncan, who I had met when I first begun the after-lunch tour, was huge but he turned out to be lovely. In a way, he reminded me of Dan. He had a big coat, long hair, and was just the way I'd wanted to be with Dan the first time I physically met him. Duncan came right up and let me fuss him. What a lovely creature. He was very happy to communicate and told me, *I'm missing my walks*. I was surprised by this. I knew that he would be restricted in terms of how far he could move about in the park, but this wasn't quite what he meant – he actually sent me a video of him walking with a collar and leash on, just like a domesticated dog. I wondered for a second if he was perhaps talking about a dog he'd seen, but this seemed to be related to him. I then spoke with Billy, as I couldn't make sense of what Duncan was sending me but it seemed so important that I didn't want to go on until it was cleared up.

'Billy,' I said, 'he's telling me that he's missing his walks, but what can that mean? He's showing me a collar and a leash, but I have no idea what's going on.'

Billy looked visibly shaken by what I was saying. 'How on earth did you know that?' he asked. 'I used to love taking him out on walks with me. We used to go really early in the morning to avoid other dogs but, because he's a dingo and has this strong natural instinct, his territorial instincts were deep-rooted and he marked a very large area for himself. He wanted to kill any other animals that were anywhere near his territory, especially domestic dogs. It was getting worse and it didn't matter how early I went out in the morning, there was always some other dog there. It got to the point where it was really dangerous. I had to stop. I had no idea the big fella missed it so much.'

I confirmed that Duncan really loved it when he used to go out with Billy, but I also suggested that I could take this opportunity to explain to him why the walks weren't happening any more. He hadn't done anything wrong – he had only been acting on his natural instinct. Poor Duncan. He was saddened by my explanation but accepting of it too; he was just lovely.

It had been quite a day but Billy had one more for me

to look at. He was particularly concerned about a dingo called Ruby, who was the mum of Rosie and Ted. I couldn't see her anywhere in the enclosure – she was actually at the very back but Billy said that she didn't come out very far, so I tuned in. Before I could get to her, Duncan came in and said, *She's a really good mum*. I said this to Billy, who agreed. I went back to tuning in with Ruby and fear came out straight away.

Absolute fear and a survival instinct, just like her daughter. She had only two things she wanted to get over to me and they came as distinct phrases as well as emotions.

Fear of man.
Need to protect my babies.
Fear of man.
Need to protect my babies.
Fear of man.
Need to protect my babies.

Ruby told me that she'd had two litters and Billy confirmed this. 'Is there anything we can do to help with the feral thing?' he asked. I tuned back in with Ruby to see if she would communicate with me.

Fear of man.
Need to protect my babies.
Fear of man.
Need to protect my babies.
Fear of man.
Need to protect my babies.

I wasn't going to get anything else from her, and nor did I think I should push. She wasn't going to change that behaviour and, while she had a lovely and trusting relationship with Billy, it had taken time to develop. Unbelievably, the next thing that happened was that Ruby came padding out and came really close to us which was, according to Billy, very unusual: he said that he'd never seen her come that close to anyone, except him – and he was in there every single day. I felt honoured and blessed to have her to come forward in this way.

I had fallen in love with these animals and this wonderful place, where the language of animals had proved to be the same regardless of the geographical distance between here and home. Now I was to experience a story that would break my heart.

Chapter 19

Simon Says

I had always wanted to visit Ayers Rock – or Uluru, as it's now known – so when we were in Australia I made a point of taking a few days out to go there with my daughter. India and I got up really early one freezing morning to go on a sunrise camel trek.

When all the camels were brought out from their pen they seemed huge and quite scary. Despite already having done this work for a few years, in me there was still part of that little girl who had been terrified of animals – and all I could remember about these creatures was what a friend who'd been on a similar trip had said about them hissing and spitting quite ferociously if they didn't take to you. The camels were linked up together and the trainers, the cameleers, told them to sit down so that the tourists could climb up, two to a camel. India was very nervous and wanted to be at the front of the line beside the cameleer, Ritchie, who would lead the trek. He was fine about that, and, after a wobbly start when the camel got up, we were on our way. As Ritchie was just in front of us, we could hear everything he was saying quite clearly and he had a lovely manner with his camel, Simon. He spoke to him very gently and chattered away naturally through-out the whole trek.

At one point, I heard him say, 'Shoosh! Get down! Shoosh!' in order to get the camels to bend their legs so that we could all get off and take pictures. Simon didn't respond, though the camels behind us did as they were told, and Ritchie tried again. 'Shoosh! Get down! Shoosh!' As clearly as anything I heard the camel's response: *Bugger off!* I had to stifle a giggle as Ritchie tried again. 'Shoosh! Get down! Shoosh!' The camel refused to budge. *Can't be bothered; same bloody routine every single morning,* came to me from Simon, who looked completely nonchalant. I laughed quietly again and tuned into him: *Are you a bit fed up?* I asked. It was almost as if he couldn't even be bothered to answer me. *As I said – same bloody routine every morning. Could* you *be bothered?* This one was quite a character.

Ritchie had pretty much given up by now, and after taking a few photos I turned my attention back to Simon. *So, what would you rather be doing?* I asked him. *What do you think? I'm hungry. I just want my breakfast.* I could understand that. *What do you have for breakfast?* I won-dered. *Melon – lovely juicy sweet melon!* he told me, and it was the first thing that he'd seemed interested in since he started talking. I tried to tune back into him and ask some more questions, but either his mind was too focused on the melon he was looking forward to or he just couldn't be bothered to reply, because that was all I got from Simon that morning.

What really interested me, however, was Ritchie's approach. He was calm and gentle, and there was no sense of him pushing this magnificent creature at all. I'd seen people get quite frustrated with their animals, especially in horse yards, and it always bothered me, so it was lovely to see how good this man was. The whole power and control thing often upsets me, particularly when people seem to think they need to show big, powerful creatures who's in charge. There was none of that here.   On the way back to the pens I wanted to say something to him both about the camel's nature and how good he'd been with him, but this kind of thing is always a funny situation. I decided to bite the bullet. 'I hope you don't mind me saying,' I began, 'but I really liked the way you handled your camel.' He laughed and said that Simon was quite the character. Ritchie had been raised with horses and used the same practices on the camels. I never come right out and say that I'm an animal communicator or animal psychic, as I never know how people are going to take things, so I was quite cautious. 'I work with animals too,' I said, 'and sometimes I get really strong feelings from them. It's not often I see such patience – I think Simon appreciated it.' He told me that he thought all animals responded to kindness and that it wasn't ever right to be harsh to them, which was music to my ears.

I was already aware that he was someone who cared for animals, so I thought it might be safe to launch into the next bit of what I wanted to say – which was what I had picked up from Simon. 'Sometimes I get really strong feelings from the animals I've worked with,' I said, 'which I've learned, through time, is like they're communicating with me.' I suppose I was trying to be subtle – hedging my bets just in case I seemed mad! 'What I got from your camel was that he wasn't being stubborn.'

This made him take notice. 'You're quite right,' he said. 'Most people get pushy or frustrated by him when he won't do things, but he isn't stubborn at all and there's no point treating him as if he is.'

'He's just a lazy thing, isn't he?' I asked.

'Yes, yes he is – you're quite right,' said Ritchie, laughing.

I laughed too. 'I don't think there's anything in his head apart from getting back so that he can have all that lovely melon for breakfast.'

Ritchie stopped and looked at me. 'How did you know that's what they get? They always get their breakfast when they return from the trek, as a reward, and they always have crates of melon.'

It was time to come clean. 'Well – he told me,' I admitted, watching the incredulous look in his eyes. 'I know, it's weird what I do, but the feelings I get are really strong and it's basically being able to communicate with animals. Your camel was telling me that he just couldn't be bothered doing this every day and he wants something juicy when he gets back.'

When we arrived back at the main centre, Ritchie asked whether I would mind having a look at some of the other camels. 'We have a couple of young ones who are new and who we're having difficulty with – maybe you could check them out?' I was delighted at the prospect. What Ritchie only told me later was that when I said I could communicate with animals, he'd thought, 'We've got a right one here,' but had figured he'd humour me. At the very least, he'd get a funny story out of the crazy Scottish woman who thought she could talk to animals! If I was actually telling the truth – and he'd been hooked by the mention I'd made of Simon's juice breakfast – then maybe I could help with the two youngsters he was really worried about. I feel it was testament to how much he cared for them that he was willing to try anything, even if it was well out of his comfort zone.

Ritchie took me to the pen where the young camels were held. It was a big, circular ring and there were two waiting – most of the others had been on the trek and were now having their breakfast. He asked me to start by looking at Bluey, who they were all a bit concerned about. As soon as I approached, he was angry. Anger can often mask other things – pain or fear being the most common – but Bluey seemed very aggressive. He told me in no uncertain terms, using words of the four-letter variety, what he wanted me to do! *Do you want to communicate with me?* I asked, only to be told where to go again. It was obvious that I wasn't going to get anywhere near him and nor did I want to, given the stories I'd heard of camels kicking, spitting and biting.

I knew that he was depressed and I was drawn to his neck, where there was a huge amount of pain, as if he'd been struck. I felt this pain myself, in my own neck, and it was agonizing. I had no doubt that he'd been abused at some point. Although he had sworn at me – and obviously that's defensive language – I felt intuitively that there was lots of emotional pain. I told Bluey that I would be back, but moved on to the camel standing beside him, who was a completely different character.

Immediately, almost at the same instant as I clicked in, she said *Hiya!* just like the bouncy dingo. Physically, the camel came no closer, but emotionally she was at me straight away. She seemed a lovely character but, within seconds, she emotionally pulled back – then came forwards again. This kept going on, as if she was saying: *Oh, I don't know about this*; then, *Yes, it's OK*; then, *I'm not sure*; then, *I really want to meet you* . . . She was back and forward constantly with her emotions. I stayed very calm and just watched these two camels for a while and actually felt that they had both suffered real trauma.

I could feel it. It was palpable, horrible. How could I tell Ritchie that these creatures felt abused? I didn't know who it was doing it and knew that I had to be very careful. Ritchie was standing watching me, so I had to say something. 'That one doesn't want to communicate,' I said, pointing to Bluey. 'He's very, very defensive and told me in no uncertain terms that he doesn't want to talk. He actually swore at me.' Ritchie nodded. 'Yes, you're spot on – he is very defensive.'

'I'm drawn to his neck,' I continued. 'There's something really bad going on there.' I still felt that he had been abused but I didn't know quite how to say so. I knew I had to find a way – my job is to advocate for animals. 'There is something that feels like trauma around his neck. I'm not accusing anyone of anything but I do feel that he's had deliberate damage inflicted on him. There's been harm on and around Bluey's neck at some point.'

Ritchie stood there quietly before saying, 'I think you're right; I've always suspected it.' I told him what I'd got from the other camel too, and he said that was perfect as well. 'This one here,' he motioned towards the young female, 'is defensive as well but there's willingness and a want to engage with people that Bluey doesn't have. The girl – she's one step forward, two steps back with people, but she does try and she'll probably be fine given time. You're absolutely spot on; I'm completely blown away.'

I told him that I was worried about Bluey. I hadn't been able to get anywhere with him because he just wouldn't let me do anything. There was such fear there. As I made to leave the camel enclosure, I asked Ritchie if I could take a picture of Bluey and work with it when I went back to my hotel room. He seemed bemused, but I guess I'd already given him evidence that I really could communicate with his animals, and know things about them that

I couldn't possibly have done otherwise, and this made him open to the idea. 'Knock yourself out,' he said. 'That little guy needs all the help he can get.' Because of Bluey's reluctance to communicate I felt that distance therapy was by far the best option for him, as there would be less pressure on the poor creature.

This felt like it was going to be one of the most important communications I'd ever done in my life.

Chapter 20

Bluey's Horror

As soon as I got back to the hotel room, I cleared my head and prepared myself for the psychic link that I hoped would come. A flood of grief washed over me as soon as I tuned in. Within seconds, tears were pouring down my face and I felt as if my heart was breaking. I often work with rescue animals and experience a range of deep emotions but I had never felt raw, unadulterated pain like this before. Bluey had been so defensive towards me when I had seen him in the camel pen, but now he had come through with heartbreaking sentiment.

It was clear that taking the photo of Bluey and bringing it back to my room was the right thing to do, because he had now opened to me straight away. In fact, the instant outpouring of pain and grief was almost a sign that he had been waiting for far too long to speak to anyone who would listen, if only they would do it on his terms.

Bluey sent me imagery of him being repeatedly struck on the neck area with what looked like a stick. He then sent an image of his legs being tied together, followed by the most incredible pain to the face and genital area simultaneously. I kept hearing the expression *Fear of man*

– it was clear that he wanted me to be in no doubt. He didn't want to move on from the initial messages. *Pain. Fear of man. Agony. Abuse.* These came through over and over again, and I couldn't help but be affected.

By this time, I'd been doing psychic work with animals for a few years. Even then my strongest tool was – as it is now – clairsentience, which is pure emotion; and with this gift I feel pain, I feel trauma, I feel upset, I feel tears. I feel all that stuff really strongly but I never actually cry. I feel the tears but they don't run because they're not mine. I'm just the tool, the transmitter that picks it up. I don't need to sit and cry; I'm just the vehicle for them to express it. That day was different. When I tuned into Bluey I had big fat tears bouncing off my chin.

Despite his great size he was just a baby. In fact, that's what Ritchie had called him – his baby. I was horrified that someone could have done these awful things to such a young animal. I sat there crying and crying, and I knew this was Bluey's grief. There was real physical pain too; a lot of rescue animals have moved beyond what has happened to their bodies and are left with emotional pain, but this was different and so very strong. When I was pulled into the neck at one point, I felt he had been absolutely battered. With the sensation I saw a close-up of the camel's neck and the image of the striking.

I sometimes feel that I am the animal with whom I'm communicating; I can feel the headache or tummy pain. But most often what I get is the imagery or the sense of things happening and I don't always feel the impact. I can measure the depth of it without always feeling it. I knew this animal had been injured deliberately. There was an image of his front legs tied together and his back legs tied together too.

As I communicated with Bluey there were very few words – it was mostly images and pictures until the end. When I saw the legs being tied, the pain I felt was incredible, as if it was my pain. I knew that this image was key to the whole trauma but for me I had no idea what it meant – for all I knew this might be a very common practice with camels. There was also the pain to the genital area and face, which I personally felt happen. As I experienced it, the agony was worse than childbirth; it was a blow, red-hot searing pain like nothing I'd ever felt before. Whatever had happened had been deliberate and with intention – it was at the root of his defensive behaviour and fear of man. Who wouldn't be fearful after something like that? However, while the injuries felt deliberate, the experience did feel old, as if it had happened before coming to this camel centre

I allowed him to show me as many images and send me as many feelings as he wanted, but they were all the same. He kept saying that he was really frightened of men, that there were three men who worked at the centre where I had met him, but that he only wanted Ritchie to work with him and definitely not the one who was *heavy-handed* with him. He wouldn't give me another name, but asked that I tell Ritchie that he liked *the game that we play with the hat*. Towards the end of our session, Bluey showed me a new picture. It was like a cartoon image of a camel lying splayed out with all four legs pointing in different directions. It was strange: despite the other awful things he had shared with me I felt there was a lightness to this message but I simply couldn't work out what it was, no matter how much I investigated. This type of message is often what is most meaningful to guardians rather than to me.

I told Bluey that I was going to help as much as I could, that I would go back and tell Ritchie all that he had passed to me, and that I was going to give Bluey a full therapy session rather than just some clearing. I did exactly that and send him lots of healing and love – but I was left with a problem. What should I do with the information I now had? I returned to the camel centre later that day, but Ritchie was out on a trek. As time passed I became more and more nervous. Bluey had said that he enjoyed his time with Ritchie and had no problems with him, but I knew nothing about the other cameleers and realized that I was perhaps about to make an accusation that could prompt things to turn very nasty.

When Ritchie returned he introduced me to the ranch manager and I wondered just what the two men would think of me. Ritchie had been supportive, but things could change. I started cautiously. One of the things I've found is that you can't just rush in and start accusing people of things based on the information you've received because your evidence needs to be strong and you need to build your case. Causing offence or upset at the beginning could put paid to them listening to any of the information that you need to share, which won't help the animal. Basically, if people feel offended or threatened they can just dismiss everything you say, which leaves the animal in the same position as they were when you started – or worse, if the abuse accumulates and causes more damage. I don't understand everything about every creature under the sun, far from it, and I sometimes find it helps if I admit to that!

'I know absolutely nothing about camels,' I began, 'so I'm sorry if this is a really daft question, but is there any situation at all in which a camel would have all four legs tied down?' The ranch manager and Ritchie the cameleer looked at each other and I saw a flicker of something pass between them – possibly recognition, I wondered.

'Why are you asking that?' the manager questioned. Again, I needed to make sure that I wasn't seen as challenging or accusing them of anything. 'Well, I'm from the north of Scotland, and we're not exactly inundated with camels up there,' I joked, 'but I do work with a lot of animals and sometimes . . . Well, I get images or thoughts from them.' I paused for a moment and looked at the two burly, no-nonsense Australian men in front of me. Of course, I'd given Ritchie an idea of what I do but I was now basically admitting that I had psychic communication with our furry and feathered friends, and had they decided to kick me out there and then I wouldn't have been at all surprised.

'You talk to animals?' the ranch manager asked. It was time to come clean.

'Erm, yes. Yes, I do,' I admitted.

They looked at each other again. Ritchie clearly hadn't given his boss much of a warm-up speech about me.

'And you've been talking to Bluey?'

'Well, no,' I began, 'I took a picture of him and went back to my hotel room, then I . . .' Even as I was saying the words, I knew that there was no way to make this sound everyday. They would either believe me or not; I may as well come clean. 'Yes,' I sighed. 'I've been talking to Bluey.'

'And he's been answering you?'

'Yes, he's sent me lots of information,' I replied, 'and he sent me this image that I can't really make sense of.'

Ritchie looked at his boss. 'She was in with the camels this morning after the trek,' he said. 'I asked her to look at the young 'uns and she was spot-on. Really – she just knew.'

I told them again about the image, all four legs tied, and this time I knew what the reaction was.

Anger.

I just had to wait and see where it would be channelled.

'I knew it!' the boss shouted. 'I bloody knew it!' It turned out that the manager had got the two young camels from

a camp in another part of Australia. He'd always suspected that they had mistreated that poor animal and that
they had used old-fashioned methods, methods that were
now considered completely outdated and cruel.

I now felt that I could give him some more information: his reaction had proved to me that he was a good
man who cared about his animals, and now I had to tell
him that things had been even worse than they seemed. I
told him that I felt the restraints had been used to prevent
the camel kicking while he was castrated and his nose
was pierced for a ring through which a harness could be
put through, and that both the piercing and his castration
had been done without any anaesthetic whatsoever. The
manager confirmed that these were among the outdated
methods he'd heard of people using. Ritchie, for his part,
agreed that Bluey just did not like anything on his head
at all; nor did he like anyone ever to raise their hand anywhere near his face – even in a totally innocent manner,
as it would be at this ranch. This was as a direct result of
the deliberate harm inflicted on his neck. Apparently it
had taken six months of daily work for Ritchie to even
hold his hand near Bluey's head.

Both men were clearly upset. I had to be very careful
about how I couched the rest of the information – it was
all very well telling them about things that had happened
to the camel in the past, but I now had to tread sensitive
ground if I was going to raise what Bluey had told me
about the other handler. 'Bluey really likes you,' I said to

Ritchie, 'and he wishes that he could just work with you all the time.'

'Not bloody likely!' said the manager. 'We're under-staffed and they're all on shifts up at the crack of dawn and then back again for sunset.'

'Well,' I began hesitantly, 'there's one other guy here who he would really rather have no contact with. I'm not insinuating that he actually mistreats Bluey but the camel has said that he's heavy-handed. Bluey just doesn't respond well to his methods.'

'Christ! I knew that as well!' said the boss, furious, as he thumped his hand against the wall. 'I should listen to my own bloody instincts! I was sure that I had seen him raise his hand to the babies but thought I must've been blinded by the sun. When I challenged him, he said it hadn't happened. Christ!'

Ritchie intervened at that point and asked what they could do for Bluey. I explained that I had done some heal-ing work with him and the very fact that he had now been heard should make a difference. 'There was one other thing – he mentioned that he liked the game you play with him.'

'What game?' asked Ritchie, kicking the dust. 'I don't play a game with him – I've never got any time.' I explained that all Bluey had told me was that they played a game every day with a hat. At this, Ritchie laughed. 'Ah! That makes sense,' he said, 'I'm not playing a game but he is! Every morning when I come in he takes the hat off my head and runs away with it round the ring. Glad I give him some entertainment!'

There was one final piece of the puzzle that I needed to work out: what did they make of the image Bluey had sent me of a cartoon camel with all four legs splayed? It seemed like a physical impossibility and I was sure it would be agony if it really happened, yet Bluey didn't seem traumatized by the image. I noticed Ritchie was smiling. 'I think I know what that is – the old fella must be listening to everything I say! I tell visitors not to go too near him 'cause he can kick out in all four directions at once!'

I returned for the last time the next day, as we were leaving. Ritchie thanked me for what I'd done but he also said that he'd had the other guy up against the wall for how he was with the camels and had handed in his resignation. He said that he was torn because he wanted to stay but felt he couldn't be around someone like that. This was hard to hear, because I knew that Bluey wanted him and needed him, but Ritchie had to make his own decisions. Both he and his boss were extremely frustrated because apparently there had already been suspicions about the other handler's behaviour. Ritchie felt there was now enough evidence for him to decide to disassociate himself entirely. I can start the healing process with animals – and people – yet I don't always know the conclusion will be. I can't fix everything and that is the frustrating part of my work.

Later there was coverage of my camel adventures in a Scottish newspaper; I never thought it would reach Australia but someone there did pick it up, which in turn led to me getting the chance to hear what had happened to Bluey. The ranch boss couldn't believe the difference I'd made to the camel: one therapy session and he was changed, apparently. The guy said that within a couple of weeks the 'magic' was unbelievable. Bluey had always hated anyone being near him and now he was out on trek with people on his back: whereas in the past he wouldn't let anyone touch him, now he wore a rein and had a chair on his back with strangers on it. Even better, Ritchie had stayed on at the ranch.

All Bluey had wanted was to be listened to – and believed. So often, it's about recognition for the animals, and so often what starts out with pain can finally end in happiness when the animal is given a voice.

Chapter 21

Sharing the Wealth

When I returned from Australia, I really felt as if a change had occurred. Although through distance communication there are no geographical limits, it had been exhilarating to have those one-to-one experiences with such different animals. Despite Bluey not actually being able to work with me in person because of his immense fear, the very fact that I had met him and seen him in the flesh was wonderful preparation for when I did do the photographic communication and healing. Being a pet whisperer was mind-blowing enough, but to have such practice with dingoes and camels was beyond my wildest dreams. Coming back to Scotland could have been a bit of a letdown, but I was determined to move onwards and upwards.

My work so far had resulted in quite a bit of media coverage, often through people contacting newspapers and radio shows, incredulous at what I'd discovered about their pets, so I now felt that it was time to take things further. If I could do this, so could anyone – it was time to take advantage of the recognition I was receiving and start spreading the message. So many animals had graciously been teaching me, it seemed the least I could do was share the wealth and pass on what I now knew.

I was very nervous before I ran my first workshop, even though I really wanted to get all of this information 'out there'. One of my posts while working in community education was as a trainer and I'd run various tailored training events for local community members as well as corporate events, so I was used to a training environment. However, this was a new subject, as well as being one of which I desperately wanted to share my knowledge and make a difference to the people who attended. My biggest fear was that I wouldn't be able to explain what I do or how I do it easily enough, or that no one would get any communication from the 'live' animal cases. Fortunately this wasn't the case. I always invite 'guest teachers' to come along to the workshops – and it's with these animals that the participants can make some striking progress.

I've never run a workshop where no one gets anything. Certainly there are those who don't get as much as they may have hoped, and who find the process more difficult than others, but that's fine. I pay particular attention to those participants so that I can highlight even the smallest piece of information they have picked up. Everyone is at different levels when they arrive, so I work really hard at ensuring no one feels left out. That's another reason why I tend to run small workshops: so that I can keep an eye on everyone and support those who may be struggling or lacking confidence or feeling frustrated with themselves. I don't want anyone to feel they have wasted their time coming to my workshop – that's important to me. What students don't always know is just how much their talent impresses and warms me.

At one event there was a woman who was reading another student's horse when she got the name of a herbal remedy that the horse said would help him. She knew nothing about herbal remedies and wasn't sure if she was even saying it correctly but the horse owner knew exactly what she was talking about.

Working with a live dog, one woman discovered that her clairsentience was clearly her strongest tool as she felt the trauma and anxiety of this poor wee pup; she was obviously deeply connected, to a degree that was tangible to me (and the other students).

One man picked up that a live horse with whom we were working was grieving the loss of a large golden-coloured companion. The horse's owner confirmed that, yes, he had indeed lost his best friend a few years beforehand. Everyone else was picking up the physical pain the horse was in, relating it to an injury, but this man had worked past that and was picking up additional issues, which was so impressive. There are often layers of information to work through, which can be difficult for novices to navigate.

I was running an animal-communication workshop in Newcastle one weekend, and had already been asked to track a missing cat who lived in that city. I had started work with the cat and was able to pass on the geography of the area, which the guardians recognized, and I used the live case as a teaching tool during the workshop. A couple of the students were spot-on with what they found and the owner was indeed able to verify the circumstances surrounding the cat's disappearance, which one student in particular had picked up quickly and accurately. This shows how information can actually be built upon by more than one communicator, and a bigger picture obtained when several communicators work together to track a missing animal.

At another workshop I ran, one woman picked up that the live rat I had invited had something grey that he loved. She said it felt like a jumper. The guardian was initially confused then realized the woman was referring to his bedding, which was partly made up of a shredded grey fleece. Information like this is detail you cannot 'guess' and it really boosts the student's confidence that the Soul2Soul Connection Technique I teach on all my workshops not only works but is also strong.

Another example of amazing specific detail being picked up on was with a live rabbit. A woman had brought her rabbit to be read by the group and I asked them to find out who its favourite person was. Unsurprisingly, everyone said the mum – except one student who said, 'a tall man with a blue waterproof jacket and glasses.' Although Mum was the favourite parent of this delightful rabbit overall, this student had described the dad perfectly

– right down to the glasses and the outdoor clothes he put on to feed the rabbit at night time. Did she get the answer wrong? Not really: the rabbit definitely preferred Dad at night, as he was the one who fed him.

I *love* running workshops and I have developed an approach that I think my clients, human and animal alike, deserve. My background and experience of training have helped me develop a strategy of sorts. For students to get the best out of my workshops I need to know my stuff inside out; recognize what I am going to be focusing on; be absolutely prepared – practically, emotionally, physically and spiritually; and have my partner, Derek, there in the background taking on all the very important but mundane tasks that are so vital to any event running smoothly – allowing me to fully concentrate on sharing my knowledge and experience with the students.

Preparation is key in this work at all levels. Time has taught me that I know enough and I trust that, too, so I can relax and go with the flow. On top of this, I have the confidence to feel absolutely OK with saying that I don't know something; it's rarely necessary but I am always honest in my teaching and with my responses – anything less would be disrespectful to my students and guests.

If, by doing all of this, I can open even one person's heart and mind to the miracle of animal communication, I can rest easy, knowing that I have passed beauty and wonder along in this world.

Chapter 22

Getting it Wrong

Do I always get it right? No. Do I get it right more often than I give myself credit for? Yes! I've had to learn to deal with the disappointment when I get something 'wrong', but actually it's usually the case that I simply haven't allowed myself enough time to unpack messages. More often than not, I've discovered that what I've thought of as my failings are actually opportunities to learn new ways of interpreting and understanding information.

Jedi's mum and dad lived locally and I would often meet them out walking my dog, Lady. They adored their family of Dalmatians and working Labradors. They were aware of the work that I did but the dad, Barry, had his reservations, and I think it's fair to say that the mum, Lindsay, had some too. However, as I've noticed so many times, people in desperate straits are willing to try anything, even those things they may have previously discounted.

Late one night, there was a knock at my front door and I opened it to find Lindsay in tears on my doorstep. She apologized for intruding but explained that she didn't know what else to do as she was so worried about Jedi, their gorgeous male Dalmatian. They had both come home from work to find him moping about, clearly in pain and unable to do the things he normally would do. They had taken him to the vet who advised that he be taken to the famous Royal Vet teaching hospital in Edinburgh first thing in the morning. This was clearly serious. Both she and her husband were worried sick and didn't know what to do. Lindsay had been quick thinking enough to bring a photograph with her and I promised that I would work with Jedi when she left, despite the late hour.

As I tuned in I felt the happy general personality of Jedi but this was quickly replaced by feelings of pain, lethargy and worry. He was clearly showing me the change in his disposition. Because this was an urgent case I quickly focused on his pain – his shoulders felt as if they were protruding, and his neck and jaw felt unbalanced too. His shoulder was clearly giving him the most agony but he told me, *I've had an injection from the vet, and the pain is bearable.*

I asked him if he knew what was happening in the morning: I wanted to talk him through the process so that he understood what to expect, thus reducing any fear he had. Yes, he did know what was happening and he talked *me* through the process, showing me an image of a scan machine too. He had clearly been listening while at the vet's.

I asked if there was anything we could all do to support him. Jedi told me he was not a good traveller and didn't like being in the car. Then he showed me an earthy-coloured red ball – but it wasn't a toy dog ball and I got the immediate impression that he was not toy orientated. *Can I have that ball with me?* he asked. *And I really want a T-shirt that belongs to my dad – I want to smell him and have him close to me.* He loved his mum and dad dearly, but he was his dad's dog. I assured him I would pass these messages on.

He was also really sad that he was such a worry to his mum and dad. I reassured him that they loved him and would do, and wanted to do, anything they could for him. Usually, if an animal is in pain I do spot clearing – that is, healing just on the area that is sore. However, in view of the seriousness of Jedi's situation, I did a complete therapy treatment on him that evening before going to bed.

I knew that Lindsay, Barry and Jedi were leaving very early the next morning for the long trip to the vet hospital so I rang them at the crack of dawn to report the key issues of the communication work and to ensure they could fulfil Jedi's requests. Before we even started talking, Lindsay said, 'I don't know what you did but Jedi's a different dog this morning.' He'd recently had difficulty climbing the stairs and most definitely couldn't jump up on their bed, which he loved to do, but that morning he had been up on the bed lavishing them with kisses. Despite his obvious pain, he was clearly feeling much better both physically and emotionally.

During the feedback they agreed that Jedi was indeed not a good traveller and they were worried about the journey. When I told them to put the ball in the car with him they were confused. 'He doesn't have toys,' Lindsay said. She called out to Barry, who was confused as well. I knew that this was important for Jedi and that he needed that ball in the car. What were we to do? Had I got it wrong? As I updated Lindsay on the rest of the communication work, Barry suddenly shouted, 'I know the ball he means. It's the cricket ball. I put it away in the cupboard years ago because I was worried he would damage his teeth on it!' I think dad was now a convert.

Jedi travelled peacefully to the vet's, the only car journey they had ever had that wasn't a traumatic experience for them all.

I tuned into Jedi the next day while he was still at the vet hospital. He was drowsy, drifting in and out of communication, but I was sure that was the anaesthetic wearing off. *I'm coming home on Saturday*, he said, but I was convinced he was wrong as I presumed they were closed on Saturdays. I shouldn't have been surprised to find out he was indeed home that Saturday evening.

The issue with the ball had irritated me. Because I was sensing that Jedi simply wasn't a 'playing' dog, I had been ready to discount his request. If Barry hadn't been open to thinking about what it could have meant, there would have been the possibility that the poor dog would have suffered a very stressful experience without the thing he most wanted to give him a little bit of comfort. It is so important to discount absolutely nothing an animal sends – and don't assume you're wrong if the guardians don't make sense of the information immediately.

Cindy, a beautiful crossbreed, had been extremely unwell for a while. I had worked with her before, with both communication and healing work, so I guess she was a regular client. Her mum, Moira, phoned me in a panic one day to say that Cindy was really unwell and deteriorating daily. Could I help? What I knew from our communication work was that Cindy was old and ready to depart this world. What I also knew was that she didn't want her mum to know this information, so it had been our secret for nearly two years. Yes, our animals hang in for us because we are not ready to let them go, and this was certainly the case with Cindy. Moira had been through an incredibly difficult and traumatic year or so and the poor dog was concerned that she just couldn't cope with any more, so was hanging on for her mum.

As soon as I tuned in to Cindy, she said, *I'm dying*. It was very clear this time. I asked her if she needed veterinary assistance and if there was anything we could do for her. *I need a yellow crystal on my bed and four amethyst crystals, one pointing to each corner of the bed.* Amethyst is a great healing crystal and has fantastic purifying and cleansing properties. I did some healing work with Cindy while her mum organized the crystals, just as she had requested. Cindy's energy and mood slowly picked up over the next few days but she was still far from right. I checked in with her daily and always got the same information: *I'm dying*. I asked her permission to discuss this with her mum and she seemed to know that the time had come. *I want to hold on for another couple of weeks but I don't know if I can*, Cindy told me. She knew that Moira had a hugely stressful time ahead as a defence witness at court and she wanted to be around to give support, not leave her on her own. I prepared Moira and we made the plans for the dog's passing according to Cindy's wishes, right down to where she wanted her ashes scattered. It was a painful and difficult time, not only because Moira was preparing to lose the love of her life, but also because she wasn't well either – she and all her animals were really unwell, tired and lethargic. It seemed to me that there was possibly something else going on here. Cindy was ready to cross the rainbow bridge, even though she wanted to stay for Moira's sake, and I wondered what the other animals were picking up.

A few days later Moira phoned me much chirpier than she had been previously. I couldn't believe it when she told me what had been going on. 'We've all had carbon-monoxide poisoning,' she said. 'That's why we've all been so ill!'

All the necessary works had been done and everyone was picking up. Why didn't Cindy tell us, Moira asked? I wondered that too, but after I had pondered it for a moment and blamed myself for not 'getting it', I realized that she *did* tell us. Cindy told me she was dying and that she had no control over it. She also needed amethyst to cleanse and purify the environment. She was dying, and she knew the air was impure – she just didn't know why.

I always teach my students that the information they receive is never wrong but that their *interpretation* of it may be. I always want to get everything right because I owe it to my animal clients, but situations like this one continually raise questions and are therefore lessons for me in how to develop my effectiveness. One of these great questions and lessons is to what extent should I use my communication skills to interfere with Mother Nature's plans.

One day I was walking Lady round the lake in our local park. It wasn't my usual morning walk – I'd decided to go there to give her a change, though I later wondered what exactly had drawn me there. As I reached the far side of the lake I noticed that one of the beautiful swans in the lake had a bleeding wing. I immediately tuned into the swan to check if he was in pain. I was immediately hit with the word *survival* and a real sense of fear. Gosh, I thought, he must be so badly injured that he thinks he is going to die. I asked him if he was in pain. *No*, he said, *no*. No? I thought he thought he was going to die; how could this be? *Survival*. *Territory*. The words came through very strongly. By this stage I had become much more adept at making connections with words and feelings, so was able to quickly establish that the key issue was territorial:

he needed to fight for his territory, hence his need for survival.

He clearly was not that bothered about his wing injury – the drive to survive was much stronger than his concern about that. However, *I* was bothered about whether he was in pain or not. He was frustrated with me and getting impatient. He quickly showed me that he had landed awkwardly and cut it but also that he was not in pain and he was not at all worried about it – it was the least of his concerns.

There was a woman watching him and we struck up a casual conversation. I intimated that I worked with animals and had a knack for picking up their feelings. I told her that he wasn't worried about his wing. She pointed over to the other side of the lake in the far corner where there was a grey-coloured swan. 'Actually, I'm more worried about him,' she said. 'Look at the state of his feathers.'

I looked again. 'Is he not one of last year's cygnets, and still grey?' I asked.

'No, it looks more like sludge,' she replied. 'They've started dredging the lake, for some reason or other, and there's not as much water.'

I was sure it was last year's cygnet so wasn't overly concerned, but something made me go to back to him and tune in. I was immediately hit with the most awful consuming sense of grief and the feeling that he needed to do that human thing of pulling over the duvet to hide from the world. It was overwhelming. He felt weak, physically and emotionally, and kept saying, *Please leave me alone*. It was heartbreaking. I can't quite explain the enormity of the 'hiding under the duvet' sensation – it was as if he was so weak and tired that he desperately needed to shut the world out and hide away; something was clearly too much for this poor wee boy.

I had no sooner started to ask him what had happened when the swan with the bleeding wing flew over from the other side of the lake and began to ferociously attack him – there was clearly nothing wrong with his wing after all. I could feel the other swan crying and felt his pain. *Please leave me*, he begged. *Please leave me alone.* It was awful. He was so weak he couldn't defend himself.

As I looked more carefully and he moved a little, I could see that the woman was right. What I taken for a grey cygnet was actually a young adult swan covered in sludge who could barely move as the larger swan continually bit him. He was pushing his head down into the water and the sludge that was just beneath the surface of the draining lake. No wonder this boy was so depressed and forlorn: he was being killed, slowly and painfully. This was something I needed help with so I phoned the SSPCA, who assured me they were on their way.

A small group of walkers had gathered and one man tipped his toddler out of the buggy and used the pram to ward off the larger swan. The noise was awful and we all felt so helpless. This poor swan just wanted to die and be left alone. I was doing all I could to hold back tears.

Soon the SSPCA arrived. Before I could reach the men

they had taken a quick look at the larger swan, who by now was back in the centre of the lake, and said his wing was fine – just clipped. People started muttering that they hadn't even examined it, but I knew they were right. By this time I was at the van and alerted them to the other swan, saying I was extremely worried about him. I didn't know how to explain what I did or what I had picked up from the swan, but I needed to do something. The men were very concerned about him too and set about rescuing him. As we chatted, I mentioned that I worked with animals and could pick up their feelings and I felt that this swan was really depressed and weak. The older of the men just looked at me and smiled – clearly humouring me. However, the other man asked what exactly it was that I did and we got talking. I was honoured that he actually invited me to get in touch with the SSPCA to offer my services.

The lesson I learned from this episode is that I only talk to animals; this doesn't mean that I know everything about them, and I would do well to remember that. I hadn't even known the second swan wasn't a cygnet. The question of whether I was right to interfere was an important one but all I know is that I could never walk past any living being that was in pain, being abused or mistreated – I would have to do something. If that means being wrong sometimes, then this is one occasion I'm happy to live with it.

Chapter 23

Tracking

One of the most difficult areas of animal communication is that of tracking. Animals, most often cats, are frequently lost or go missing and, while I try to help as often as I can, this is not only time-consuming but also very emotional work. Sadly, the outcome isn't always successful, because it might take a while before human companions get in touch with me, during which time the animal may have become weaker or even passed over. Sometimes animal psychics are seen as a 'last resort' for people wishing to find their missing pet – my life, their happiness and the safety of their beloved pets would be much easier and secure if they came to me at the outset.

The case of Jasper the missing cat was one of the most troubling of my career – as well as being the one that almost made me give up. All I had was a photograph, sent by email, and the most basic of facts: Jasper had been missing for a week. I began by carrying out a brief tune-in to establish whether he was still alive. I emailed his dad to say that I would endeavour to communicate with him every day until he was found. With that first tune-in I was immediately bombarded with a series of images and

220

words: *Edinburgh, canal, terraced houses*. I was shown a route over a bridge that passed over water. There seemed to be steps at the bridge and I assumed that the water was the canal to which Jasper was referring. He sent me images showing him turning right once over the bridge before taking a left turn. Here, the area seemed to be built up and it felt as if there were rows of houses on either side of the road.

I then immediately received the word *meadow* and saw an image of a large, green space with trees down one side near a road and houses across that road. Later, I felt as if there could have been some swings too. In the email to his dad, Jim, I asked whether that description was familiar, as I really needed some feedback to know whether I was getting the right messages.

Jasper was feeling scared and desperately wanted to get home. He asked me to get his dad to come for him: he wanted him to call for him at midnight that night. I didn't feel that he was injured – in fact, he seemed very well; his main concern was his appearance. He was a beautiful cat but he felt that he was a mess at the moment, and very dirty.

Towards the end of my time with him I saw a hospital sign very clearly. I felt that it could have been close to the meadow that he described, and that, although he said he was far from home – about two miles – this sort of information can be misleading. I had learned from other tracking cases that 'far' is a very subjective term for cats and can mean anything, depending on the distance they would normally travel. In fact, the previous cat I had tracked had told me he was *miles and miles* from home when he was actually only ten minutes away. He never usually left the immediate vicinity of his house, so it was actually *miles and miles* for him.

I sent a couple of emails and left a message for his dad because I needed to find out what was happening – even whether Jasper had been found and whether I should keep trying. In fact, he'd sent me a message at one point that said his dad had picked him up from the vet, which seemed very specific, and I was desperate to find out if that was true.

Jim's reply wasn't very helpful in the sense that he didn't tell me whether I'd been accurate or not. He simply said: 'Thank you for your email and call. There is a lot I want to write to you. However, I do not want to do it right now.' This did seem a little odd to me, as there was nothing in it for me to go on. I kept tuning in, and emailed again a few days later to point out that, 'Obviously if the geography I have described is accurate or inaccurate then that is essential to know. I know this is a difficult and emotional time for you but please feel assured that I will do my utmost for Jasper.'

After a week I still hadn't heard anything so I left another phone message, hoping that this poor man wouldn't think I was stalking him. I told him that I really needed some feedback if I was to continue tracking, and that at our last session he had moved on from where he was to begin with and said that he was back home.

I was stunned by Jim's reply. 'Geographically, your images are all correct and the route you describe is Jasper's territory. The only problem is that he is dead.' Oh no! Apparently Jasper had died the day before I started tracking him. Jim been on holiday and hired a cat minder to look after Jasper and his little brother, Pickle. This person had lied about the last time she had seen Jasper. Jim had later found out that Jasper had been found at the bottom of some steps leading to the offices of what was known as the Canal Society of Edinburgh on the Sunday morning. Jasper had apparently spent a lot of time near this bridge and at the Canal Society itself.

As he put it: 'I got a phone call telling me what had happened to my lovely cat. We think he had been hit by a car and crawled down the steps to die. A very kind gentleman from the Canal Society had buried him on the banks of the canal. He's in a very beautiful spot, a spot where he spent a lot of his time chasing ducks, but I wish he was still here with me. Do I know it's definitely him? Yes, we had to dig him up to confirm or I would always have expected him to come home. Pickle has been missing him terribly. There has been a terrible emptiness in the house.'

I was so confused by it all, as well as being upset. I had been happily communicating with this cat for days and not even recognized that he was dead. This was why he hadn't wanted to go into any detail in his first email: he'd been grieving, and I'd been telling him that I'd had messages from his cat. Some things did make sense – he was worried about his appearance because he'd been in an accident, and he'd been buried, so he was covered in dirt. However, he was sending me information that supported him being on earth. Jim also told me that the location markers I'd got were spot on and that he lived about two miles from where he was found.

So, I was torn. Yes, I was pleased that I had got the location absolutely right, but I was horrified that I hadn't picked up on Jasper's passing ... Until a further message from Jim made everything very clear. He had gone into the local vet's practice to take down the 'missing' poster and the lady there had been sympathizing with him, having known Jasper quite well. She told Jim that they had an abandoned kitten who was awaiting transfer to the local cat sanctuary, and maybe the acquisition of a new cat would help Pickle's grief. Jim was, at first, horrified at the very idea of getting a new cat so quickly after his loss – it wasn't as if Jasper could be replaced. Grudgingly, he went to look at the kitten – and couldn't believe his response to it. He immediately felt drawn to the poor little thing as if he already knew it, and adopted Dennis there and then.

Now, here is the amazing part of the story. The new kitten had been found near the Meadows, a public park in Edinburgh, with swings at one end and trees bordering the road. There are terraced houses nearby and all this is visible from the Canal Society offices where Jasper had been laid to rest. At the Meadows stands the site of the old Edinburgh Royal Infirmary – hence the hospital sign Jasper had sent me. Could it possibly be that soul transference had taken place and that Jim's immediate link to Dennis was because his old beloved cat was now part of him? It was amazing but I was learning to be open to everything and anything. All I could intuit was that, after dying, Jasper had taken a route from the steps where he was knocked down, which then led him over the bridge and to the park, where Dennis had been found, alone and desperate. From what I had researched, soul transference can happen when an animal passes suddenly and is either not prepared for it or unaware that they are now dead: their soul can transfer to the body of another animal.

Jim said he felt that Jasper was *still around* and even that he often felt he'd seen him out of the corner of his eye, only to realize it was his new cat – even though they were physically very different. It all fitted together beautifully and I could finally see why Jasper had told me that he was still alive and his dad had gone to the vet to collect him: because, he had. I was very wary about telling Jim all this, because it wasn't as if Jasper had come back exactly – Dennis was a different cat, he just had the essence of Jasper within him – but I did ask him to look and see if there was anything he recognized in him and to take comfort from Dennis.

I was so very close to giving up at one stage of the Jasper story. I had convinced myself that I was terrible at this work, and even managed to discount every other successful communication I'd ever had. How could I possibly risk getting things wrong again? Once the story sorted itself out and I realized that soul transference may have taken place, I 'got back on the horse', so to speak, and my goodness was I glad of that, for the next missing cat situation I dealt with was so wonderful that it put everything back into perspective.

One afternoon I got a terribly distressed call from a woman called Leyla to report that her tiny kitten, Peanut, had been missing for five days. I immediately felt that the cat didn't go out often and wasn't far from home. Leyla confirmed that Peanut went out only every few days. In view of this, and of how long she had been missing, I was extremely concerned. I just knew (with the claircognisance kicking in) that Peanut wasn't far from the house. The kitten disagreed and told me she was far from home – probably because she was the furthest from home she had ever been. She was petrified. With tracking work I always try to tune into the lost animal as soon as their mum or dad gets in touch – time is of the essence and I need the communication to begin immediately.

As Leyla and I spoke on the phone, and as I continued the communication with Peanut at the same time, I received an image that led me down the front path of the house, through the gate and took a left turn. There was a row of houses opposite but I felt the sensation of a field. When I described the location to the Leyla she agreed that it was her street and there was a field at the bottom of the road if a left turn was taken. Peanut told me that she had got a fright outside the front of the house and had just ran.

I knew the field was going to be vital to Peanut's rescue so concentrated on receiving information about that. I saw the image of a pylon, which felt significant, and asked if there was indeed a pylon at the entrance to the field on the right-hand side and bushes by a path on the left side. Leyla said that, yes, there was, but the lefts and rights were wrong; fair enough, I must be seeing it from the opposite side. I already knew that Peanut was dirty and scared and I now felt that she was trapped. This was a strange sensation, because she did not feel trapped in, behind or underneath something; it was more of her feeling trapped in general. In view of the fear I could feel from her, I determined that she was indeed trapped but that this was an emotional rather than physical situation: she was trapped by her own fear. I could also feel earth and roots – she was hiding, rooted by her fear, in the bushes.

Leyla said she would go to the field straightaway so I told Peanut to meow as soon as she heard her mum call her. But just as I was passing that message on I stopped. Something didn't feel quite right; she felt vocally quiet.

I asked Leyla if Peanut was a vocal cat and she said she wasn't. There was no point in me asking her to meow, then, as she would be too quiet to do that. Animals often just 'wait' to be rescued and don't always realize they need to help as well, and often need specific instructions. I now knew that Peanut would not or could not meow loudly so I sent her an image of what she would need to do. I sent a beam of white light from the bushes to the pylon and told her to follow that light and wait for her mum at the pylon itself.

I prepared Leyla for disappointment, as animals are so rarely found on the first communication and it is often like piecing together a huge jigsaw puzzle in the dark. Additionally there was something about this that just didn't feel right, and, despite the feeling I had that Peanut had picked up and understood my instructions, I wasn't convinced that Leyla would find her. I wasn't surprised when she phoned a little while later to say that Peanut was not there and that she couldn't find her anywhere in the field, though she had searched for ages. I reassured her that I would keep working with her kitten when her front doorbell rang and she had to hang up.

She called me back about two hours later, hysterically happy. She told me that the knock on her door while we'd been on the phone earlier had been a neighbour who was worried about Peanut and was wondering if she was home yet. Leyla had told her that she was optimistic, because a pet whisperer was doing some communication work at the moment. The neighbour promptly pooh-poohed the notion and told her she was wasting her time.

The neighbour left to go to the nearby local shops. Apparently this was a straight route from A to B, but, for some very strange reason, the neighbour had come back a completely different way – which was longer and which she had never taken before. (With hindsight I'd probably say there wasn't a 'strange reason' at all – these things have a way of working that I don't always understand but that I always respect.) The detour took her through a field, a different field to the one previously mentioned, with bushes down the path and a pylon at the exit. Who was sitting at the pylon? None other than Peanut. Ravenous, dirty but unharmed – and desperate to get home to her mum, for whom she'd been waiting so very long at the pylon.

During my discussion with a jubilant Leyla claircognisance kicked in, with the shiver down my back informing me that Leyla was never meant to find Peanut, as I now suspected – the neighbour was. The most probable reason for this was to open her eyes to a world of information that she hadn't known about or believed existed. I felt drawn to the woman's heart and felt she was more open to animals than people. Leyla confirmed that in the eighteen years she had lived next to the woman they had rarely exchanged much more than pleasantries, and had never been in each other's house. After finding the kitten the neighbour invited Leyla and her children over for a celebratory drink – animals truly can help open hearts and minds.

Chapter 24

Messages from the Heart

After Jones, but long before Peanut, I was drained. Physically, mentally and emotionally, I needed some quiet time. I didn't have many animal communication clients waiting to be dealt with, and I was busy with everything else in my life. I wasn't scared or worried about it in any big way because I had been going through lots of other things, including a divorce and a house move, which meant that my stress levels were going through the roof. Although I was still communicating, I didn't think I was reaching the level I usually did – in short, I was disappointed with myself and decided to put all communication work on hold.

One summer evening I was out on a walk, trying to clear my mind and think things through. I didn't know the area well, having moved there only a few months before, and the communication 'block' was really getting to me. As I was walking with my collie, Lady, I saw a deer, then quickly realized there were actually three of them. All I thought to begin with was, *How beautiful.* This was a really nice bit of wooded land that I'd been drawn to but hadn't seen before. I looked at the deer and thought, *Right, Sarah-Jane, if you think you can communicate with animals, get on with it and try these for size.* I needed to see what would happen but it was also a ridiculous task to set myself. I really had no expectations: they were wild animals, I wasn't tuned in for working, I was worried about my abilities and in nowhere near the right frame of mind to do it, but I stood there and did a bit of grounding work before connecting.

We're lost, was all I got.

That was hardly earth-shattering – anyone could have come up with that looking at three deer quite close to a road. You didn't need to be an animal communicator to work that one out and I was already doubting what I was getting. They came through again: *We're lost, we're lost.* Then, *Can you help us, please?* I didn't even know how they'd got there so how could I tell them to get out? I had no knowledge of the location at all. The only thing I knew was that there was a really busy road behind them. I sent the words, *Don't go through those trees; there's a busy road back there and you're likely to get killed.* I sent an image of what would happen – a graphic, horrible one of them getting run over – as well as a positive one of them running to safety if they went in the opposite direction. During this, I was telling myself that I was really just having some mental chatter going on and that it was a conversation with myself, not a four-way communication with the deer.

For some reason, I started to tell them this as well: I

confided in them that I was having a block and was actually beginning to doubt whether I had any skill at this at all. I said to them that all I was getting was general stuff that anyone could have guessed, then told them, *Right, you're going to have to help me here.* I focused on one in particular. *If I'm really communicating with you, I need you to take a couple of steps to the right and then I'll know this is real, that I'm actually communicating.* They were all munching on the grass, not looking at me, then, one by one, they stopped and individually eyeballed me. Every single one was standing there looking directly into my eyes! It was quite amazing even having that experience never mind that it was because of the communication work. All three of them looked at me, very calmly, then I swear that they moved – not to the right, but to the left. I thought, *I knew it, I knew I couldn't do this.* Then it occurred to me that my right was their left. They had done what I had asked them! How could that have happened? Deer wouldn't just stop eating grass, one by one, then all move as a group a few steps in one direction together in a simultaneous movement while still watching me. They stayed there for a while as I sent them lots of love, lots of pink light, then they moved away, keeping away from the direction I'd told them was the busy road.

It absolutely reinforced my faith in what I was doing and allowed me to recognize that not only does ego get in the way of communication work, but so does stress. I had gone through some major changes in my life and, although positive, they were still highly stressful. I gave myself permission to have a couple of days off work to recharge my batteries then fell back into it all full swing again. Occasionally there are little blocks, and I now embrace them as gentle reminders that I need to take time out and re-charge.

Messages from the heart can be sent and received, but sometimes the stories that come through are positively heartbreaking. Thankfully, the capacity of animals to love is bigger than the ability of humans to hurt them, and for that we should all marvel. One day, I was contacted by a dog behaviourist called Julia who was extremely worried about a German shepherd-cross puppy who would later be named Dylan once he had a loving home. She had been contacted by a woman who lived on a farm near to her and who was extremely concerned about the health of this dog. When Julia went there to investigate, the farmer made it clear that he couldn't be less interested – in fact, he didn't even have a name or collar for Dylan because he never paid him any attention. When Julia said that she would like to take the dog and find him a home, he told her she was welcome to him and left without even looking back.

Dylan was taken to the home of the woman who had initially contacted Julia with her concerns, and Julia suggested that this lady contact me as she thought the dog might have some issues, having been badly treated and now placed in a new home so suddenly. Julia called me to tell me to expect a phone call and, while I was talking to her, I was immediately connected to Dylan. A flood of emotions came through, all intense, all overwhelming: *Fear, abandonment, anxiety, defensiveness, timidity.* The very root of him, his soul almost, was completely shot to pieces. This poor dog had no stability or grounding, no family or place in the world. I sensed he could trust no one, but that he wasn't a bad dog – far from it. I didn't know at this stage what had happened to him, but I knew it was bad. I had never felt such disconnection before – from his environment, from all other beings, from his own emotions. Dylan was in a bad way.

That night I tuned in again, as I just couldn't get him out of my mind, and began piecing together his story. The key issues he shot through to me were: *Separation, lack of nurturing, physical abuse.* The root of all of these issues was the loss of his mother and he was totally closed down emotionally as a result. The images and feelings Dylan was sending me were horrific – he'd been so badly beaten that blood had been drawn on numerous occasions and he desperately wanted to reach out to someone but there was never anyone there who cared for him. How can people do these things to animals? He was just a baby.

Julia looked into Dylan's background as I continued to work with him. When we put both of our investigations together, the history was dreadful. Dylan had been one of a litter of six born on the farm from which he had been rescued. The mother had not been checked on at all during her labour and had died either during or just after childbirth. The pups were left alone, freezing and unable to feed. When they were found the following day, they were near dead and the farmer instructed his wife to dump them all in the bin. She didn't – to her credit, she took them indoors and warmed them up. Some did survive, but as soon as the remaining ones showed some sign of improvement they were housed in the barn again. I can't stress strongly enough how awful it was for them to be placed back at the scene of their mother's death, alone and without nurturing: the damage was immeasurable.

I didn't know what had happened to most of the others (they were probably sold) but I was soon to learn the fate of one. As soon as Julia mentioned that Dylan's sister was there, I had the most awful feeling . . . As if she was dying. I told Julia that, like Dylan, the sister was completely disconnected from her surroundings but that for her this disconnection was so great that she was dying, emotionally and physically. This dog actually felt nearly dead to me. She had completely shut down and had lost the will to live.

Julia is a wonderful, warm woman, completely devoted to animals, and she rushed to the farm, where she found Bonnie (as she would be called) in the same old barn with another dog. The other dog was food aggressive and had clearly been preventing Bonnie from eating, as she was woefully thin. It transpired that the farmer knew this and just shrugged it off when challenged by Julia with the suggestion that he had deliberately allowed a puppy to be denied food in the likelihood that she would starve to death. Julia removed Bonnie and found her a loving home.

I did some distance-healing work with both dogs and they both responded fantastically well. To begin with, Dylan was unable to show affection because he had shut down emotionally – he didn't know how to react at first, and was very wary. He's now a changed dog: the grief has been removed, he knows that his sister is well and for the first time in his short life he has a sense of belonging. I recently received an email from Dylan's new mum to say that he had come on to her bed for the first time and was cuddling into her.

There are healing techniques that are very effective when I work with animals, many of which come from the ancient ways of living and learning that I referred to earlier. The notion of the body having different chakras (or energy centres) is something which has become very popular recently as many of us try to reconnect with old wisdom. Animal chakras are in approximately the same place as ours but working on them is different to working on those of people. The first dog I ever I worked on, Gregory the Labrador, had lots of shoulder problems. There were physical manifestations of this but I believed they were coming from the heart chakra, which is where we store grief. There was a lot of upset in Gregory's life, much of which had to do with responsibility: he was literally shouldering a lot of responsibility. When I checked this out with his mum, she confirmed that she put pressure on him. He was a show dog and she had certain expectations of him – as he did of himself – but she had been unwell recently and he had felt that he'd 'looked after' her. This had meant that he didn't really want to perform; he was tired and he also felt his new role as carer was more important.

There is a beautiful technique to get deep into old residual grief and really get it pulled out. You go into the heart energy centre, locate the blockage and gently raise it up to the shoulder and then pull it down the arm and away from the body. People usually have to hold their arm out to facilitate this process. I knew that I needed to do this technique with Gregory the dog but I wondered how I could get him to do what a person would do. He barely sat still for five minutes – I certainly couldn't get his 'arm' out at ninety degrees.

He and his mum had come to me for a one-to-one consultation and I'd said to the woman that it was perfectly fine for Gregory to wander around and not to mind if I closed my eyes. Although we were in the same room, I'd do it as a distance session. I sat down, closed my eyes and just imagined that he was standing up on his back two legs like a person with his front legs outstretched like arms. Another successful technique for cleansing the system of old debris requires the person to sit on a chair with their legs outstretched. I did that too in my mind with Gregory – and it worked. His mum reported that, after that session, he was free of his physical symptoms and a much happier dog. She'd also agreed to keep him away from his show duties for a while, until he indicated to me that he was ready to return. When I passed this information on to Gregory, the sense of relief was palpable – his heart was lighter, he had been listened to and his needs had been met.

What animals can teach us about the power of forgiveness and the ability to mend hearts is remarkable. I never cease to be amazed at how absolutely thoughtless and cruel some people are. Thankfully, Dylan and Bonnie have moved on to much happier lives, and Gregory was in a good place to begin with. I can't help or heal every animal – but I'm happy to do it one at a time.

Chapter 25

Mirroring and Healing

Not all cases come to a swift conclusion. I'm dealing with life and all the breathtaking complexities of it, which means that patience (thanks again, Barney!) is one of my most treasured tools.

The story of Breeze, a beautiful chestnut stallion, took more than a year to unfold but it shows so well how animal communication information sometimes makes no sense when it occurs, or takes time to come to human understanding. Helen contacted me about communicating with her horse in 2008, as she was having problems riding him and he had begun headshaking. I immediately received the word 'neuralgia' and felt that he was having difficulties with his back and legs; he seemed absolutely exhausted but I couldn't put my finger on there being anything physically wrong. The symptoms clearly weren't imaginary, yet it was almost as if he was feeling these things but they weren't part of him. It was beginning to feel like the familiar 'mirroring' going on. Sensitively, I had to ask Helen whether she had any of these symptoms herself.

People come to me expecting to have things relating to

their animal addressed, but these can't always be separated from what is going on for the guardian. When I fed back that Breeze's exhaustion in the back legs felt related to her, she confided in me that she had multiple sclerosis and that many of the things I was telling her about Breeze were identical to her own symptoms. About six months after our first contact, he underwent an operation on the trigeminal nerves in his face – the very nerves that cause headshaking and neuralgia. He didn't respond well to the operation. The professor who performed it said that he had the equivalent of MS without a shadow of a doubt, as his balance was affected and everything seemed more connected to the central nervous system.

Breeze's ongoing medication is the same as that for Helen, and she also treats him homoeopathically – again, like she does herself. Almost a year after we first communicated she rode him for the first time in eleven months and he was a calm, contented horse. Helen sees his symptoms differ from day to day, just like her own, and even though some days he looks perfect, she judges his capabilities by her own health and energy levels.

Clearly Breeze and his mum had a strong physical and emotional connection with each other and had a truly loving bond, which was beautiful to see. Both now take each day as it comes, and no one understands each other the way they do. In Helen's words, 'I am so glad that we found each other. Breeze has changed my life. The love and strength I feel from him makes him so special to me.' Many animals themselves are talented healers and, like Breeze, support their human companions by mirroring their symptoms and sharing their pain so they can help heal them. Breeze and Helen's love and commitment to healing each other meant they found a way through the pain together.

When I dealt with a seventeen-year-old cat called 2sox, I was amazed by the three-way healing process he created between him and his mum, Mary, and a neighbour too. 2sox had a long-term history of spraying both in and out of the house. The continual spraying was causing concern for Mary, who was incredibly frustrated with it and was becoming increasingly worried as her neighbours were complaining about the mess and smell.

Mary hadn't given me any background other than this, but when I reported my findings to her she was astonished. 'I couldn't believe how much you could know about the life of 2sox,' she told me. 'You accurately detailed a time of great loneliness for him and you were also able to identify how many rehomings he'd had – three before he came to me.' 2sox had told me that Mary *feels like Mum; I love her as my mum; I'm happy there – but I'm not 'her' cat*. I picked up that he identified very strongly with a man in his life and that was where his primary loyalty lay. I didn't quite understand this, but it was what 2sox was telling me. He told me that this man was very ill and that *Mum needs to see him; she knows him already*.

This was fascinating and I asked Mary to give me a little

more background if she recognized what 2sox was talking about. She immediately did. The man to which the cat had referred was called Harry, a neighbour of Mary's. Harry had previously been one of 2sox's guardians, but was no longer looking after him as he had cancer and was very ill. Despite being ill, Harry was no good at asking for help. It now became clear that 2sox was spraying out of frustration and to get Mary's attention. He was trying to tell her that something was wrong with Harry. 2sox was acting as nothing less than this man's health interpreter and looking for a way to get Mary to take notice and check on Harry.

Harry was such a proud man that he would never say if he was feeling ill or in pain, but 2sox had such a strong connection with him that *he* knew if Harry's health was getting worse or if he needed help. It was this that caused him to spray.

As a result of the communication and what 2sox told me, all parties accepted that this wonderful cat was indeed Harry's health indicator. Harry gave Mary a key to his flat so that she could check on him any time and 2sox now alerts her on the days that aren't so good for Harry. It was just marvellous to see how loyal and connected 2sox was with Harry; he made a real difference to his health, making sure that Mary could help Harry when he needed it.

While acting as a health interpreter was the main reason for 2sox's spraying, it was also linked to a long-term urine infection he'd had when living at a home before Harry or Mary. He told me that he'd had this for *three years*. I felt there was residual damage left over from that time and that a course of healing therapy would help. A combination of this and the recognition of his role as Harry's health indicator saw him become pain free and the spraying stopped completely – apart from on one occasion when, as a result of him starting again, Mary hurried to Harry's flat only to find him in desperate need of help and in terrible pain.

For me, the outcome of the 2sox story was a win/win situation all round. Mary had longed to take this cat into her care, and was now providing him with lots of love; 2sox's loyalty to Harry had been served through the patience and sensitive nature of Mary; and, last but by no means least, Harry has his guardian angel looking out for him at all times.

I was someone who had never really been seriously ill, so the physical side of the work I was doing wasn't something I could necessarily relate to – but I learned a lesson one day many years ago before my life as a pet whisperer. I was close to a neighbour of mine called Delia. One weekend, she was meant to be involved in fronting an event but on the morning she should have been driving to it she couldn't even get out of bed. She phoned me and asked if I could pop in, without telling me what was the matter.

'What's wrong?' I asked her, as she groaned in agony after opening the door to me. 'It's my head,' she answered. 'I've got the most awful migraine.' I knew that she did suffer from blinding headaches and that when they came they were often debilitating. 'I'm going to have to cancel this blasted event,' she said. As I looked at her, I knew she was right.

I'd followed her into her bedroom and once she'd lain down she couldn't even lift her head off the pillow. She was talking in a whisper. 'OK, where are the contact details? I'll call them for you. What's the number?' I asked.

Delia groaned again. 'I don't have any,' she said. 'I don't have a number or anything. There's nothing I can do, though – there's no way I can go, so they'll just have to do without me. They'll realize I'm not turning up eventually.' There were so many people planning to attend this event and they were all going to be waiting for her. If no one knew that she wasn't going to turn up, there would be no opportunity to arrange for someone else to host it and the whole day would be disorganized and ruined. I wouldn't have been able to do that; I'd have dragged myself in no matter what. But then I'd never had a migraine and I couldn't really imagine just how bad the pain was. This must have been bad, for Delia to be pulling out, as she was usually such a conscientious person.

I went downstairs to get her some painkillers. There was a little niggling voice in my head that wouldn't go away. I'd had various aches and pains of my own sorted when I was at healing workshops – maybe I could do it? Maybe I could get rid of the migraine. 'Delia?' I said when I went back to her. 'Don't take the tablets yet; I want to try something.' She was in such agony that she didn't really say anything as I sat down beside her on the bed. I placed my hands over her as had been done to me at reiki, and in my head I kept saying, 'Please take this headache away, please take this headache away,' over and over again.

I didn't really know what else to do, so after a few minutes I stopped. 'Delia?' I whispered. 'How do you feel?' She said nothing. I suppose I wasn't that surprised. Anything had been worth a go, but I also knew that people trained for years to become healers and they knew a whole lot more about it than I did, so it was pretty unlikely that I would have managed to 'fix' Delia. I stood up and headed for the bedroom door, thinking that I'd just leave her there to recover, hoping that the pain might ease as the day went on. 'Sarah-Jane?' she said, as I walked away. 'Get my coat, will you? Looks like I'll be going after all.'

I could hardly believe what I was hearing! 'What?' I said. 'Are you feeling a bit better?'

'A bit better?' answered Delia. 'I'm absolutely fine, love – it's gone. The migraine's completely gone. I've no idea what you did, but it worked. I feel fantastic.'

I didn't quite know what I'd done, either, but as she left for the event I was walking on air. All that mattered was that she felt better and, somehow, I'd achieved that. I waved goodbye and wondered what I'd do with the rest of my day, given that I felt so good.

It didn't last.

I'd never had a migraine in my life – in fact I'd rarely even had a bad headache – but within minutes of Delia leaving and me going back to my own house, I felt as if I was going to collapse with the blinding pain pulsing through my forehead. My scalp and skull felt as if there was a crushing weight, and the agony kept increasing. I had to lie down – and I couldn't get up for the rest of the day; there was no way I could have stood on my own two feet. When Delia came back from her event she rushed into my house, our doors being always open to each other. I was still in bed. 'I still feel great!' she said, bounding in. 'What a day – I feel better than I have in years.' She stopped to look at me, lying in the dark, hardly able to speak.

'I think I've got your migraine,' I muttered, every word draining me. 'I've taken it on.' I collapsed back into darkness, and had no other option but to wait for it passing. It was a rookie mistake, really. What I had done for Delia had worked, but I needed to learn to do these things properly if I was ever to risk doing them again. Before I did that with Delia, I had been disrespectful of my natural healing powers – even if I had used them with the best of intentions. When that migraine incident happened all those years ago, I knew without doubt that I had the ability to do healing work, that I had that natural ability, but this was a wake-up call telling me that I needed to know the rules to keep me and anyone I worked with safe. This was vital if I wanted to develop my ability to heal. That was when I made the decision to train professionally in therapy work.

Reflecting on my journey, I see that there were so many occasions where lessons and opportunities were presented to me that I didn't necessarily recognize as such at the time. For example, the migraine incident all those years ago, which evidenced that I could 'heal' but taught me the importance of not being flippant about it and demonstrated how important it was to understand what I was doing and why. This led to working with and understanding animals at a deeper level, recognizing when animals were genuinely ill or when they were mirroring their guardian's ailments. Working with the gifts I had been blessed with, I could help animals heal by supporting their guardian's return to health; and, in turn, I could help guardians heal by supporting their animal's return to health.

Chapter 26

Goldie's Trauma and Merlin's Pride

Goldie was a stunning palamino stallion. Bred in the Netherlands and imported into the UK, he was a well-known stud and show stallion over there before coming to his mum, Audrey.

Audrey got in touch with me because both she and her daughter were incredibly troubled about their gorgeous boy. They both felt his behaviour had changed hugely and the vet couldn't find anything wrong with him. They were worried sick.

I remember saying to them after the first session that Goldie certainly made me work hard for everything and it was a little like pulling teeth. This does sometimes happen because an animal is shy or reserved, but with Goldie I felt it was less to do with that and much more to do with his mood and how he was feeling.

What's the matter, Goldie? I asked. *Change,* he shot back. The change felt emotional in origin rather than physical, and that he was grieving the loss of someone. I felt he was sad, had lost his spark and was closing down internally. This was all related to the bereavement process he was going through. He sent me the words, *Baby, I miss*

249

my baby. I needed Audrey to give some thought as to whether there had been a change in his field companions and to consider whether there was a girlfriend or a foal or younger horse in which he took an interest.

He didn't really want to talk, but I felt there was a strong love connection behind his low mood. I was sure his loss was attributable to the loss of a girlfriend. I felt that he was an incredibly sensitive soul (both emotionally and physically) and that the impact of these losses was affecting him greatly.

I was drawn to his tummy area and felt that he could be off his food as his tummy felt a little off balance. I was also drawn to his throat which was congested (most probably due to unexpressed emotion). His mum confirmed that it could be difficult to get Goldie to communicate – she joked that it was maybe a language problem because he had come from Holland.

Audrey agreed that he was indeed a tricky character, who pretended to be big and bold but was really very sensitive and took everything to heart, retreating inwards with his emotions, only to blow up on occasion. He was totally frozen and zoned out when he first came to Audrey and her family and it took a few months for him to trust and adapt to his new life and even enjoy it.

Her next words were vital to understanding Goldie: 'You are spot on with "baby". I thought he was grieving for his mare and foal – he was kept with them all summer, but had to be separated at the start of October as they were going back to Holland. He was particularly close to the foal – not his foal, but he had been with her ever since she was born in May. He went down to livery at the start of October, where we are keeping him over the winter, and bringing him back into work and doing some competitions. It has been difficult for him lately there as they have brought all the foals in and weaned them, so that has likely caused him distress as they are stabled just across from him. If you could tell him that Rebus (the foal) and Wonder (the mare) were safe and sound in their new homes in Holland that might help?'

When I next tuned into Goldie, I sent him all of this information. I was particularly keen to emphasize that, *Rebus and Wonder are safe and sound. You need not worry about them.* He was still grieving for the mare and foal, and I felt this as a psychic shiver, so I wasn't sure whether my words about them being safe and sound would be enough or whether he was in the right place to take my advice about behaving better. *Fine. But tell them I don't need two riders. I need Audrey.* I said that I would pass it on, and asked whether there was anything else. *Yes – tell her she's good. She shouldn't lose confidence – we'll get there.*

I told Audrey that I found Goldie incredibly closed emotionally and that it felt psychological in origin. She was in complete agreement and described how 'frozen' he was when she got him and long it had taken her to work with him. I advised her that he was very sensitive and often seemed to feel as if he was being worked heavy-handedly

251

but that this was because of his incredible sensitivity, not his guardians, who used natural-horsemanship methods. Having two riders had been causing him confusion. He needed a strong, calm leader and Audrey was the best person for that job, which was why he had chosen her. It transpired that she had some health problems and, despite being a competent rider, had lost confidence in riding Goldie he had bucked and thrown her daughter so many times. She could not physically take any more risks, but when I told her that Goldie 'promised' me that he would be gentle with Audrey if only she would take control and ride him (and therefore heal him), she was very touched and agreed to try. This would be their journey together, I felt with another psychic shiver. I could make no guarantee – it had to be her choice – but I did feel that Goldie really wanted to try.

In my next session, I kept assuring Goldie that the foal and mare were safe and happy in Holland. Although he felt like the father, that foal was not actually his, and Audrey suggested that he try and get to know another foal, who was also at the yard. I immediately felt Goldie had no connection with this foal and told Audrey this. She was not surprised. Apparently the mare had fought Goldie any time he tried to get near her or the foal. A little more work identified that Goldie would like to make a connection with the foal, but it would all take time.

He had been overworked in Holland at stud and Audrey told me that if they could not 'fix' him he would need to go back, as the Dutch people had half ownership. Claircognisance told me he absolutely did *not* want to go back there, so I had to tell him in gentle but clear terms that if we couldn't find a way to resolve these issues he would need to go back. He asked for more therapy work, which I did after the communication.

Goldie also had what I would call 'male issues'. I kept picking up that he had a strong female side and that was probably key to his oversensitivity. However, each time this raised itself he told me that he was strong and powerful and could hold his own ground easily if he needed or wanted to. There was clearly a real need for him to 'prove' this or have it heard, as he kept saying that others thought he was *dainty* or *feminine* and he didn't like it. When I told Audrey this she laughed and said he was far from dainty but everyone called him 'gay' because of his fabulous colour and good looks. Again there was a shiver and I just knew that Goldie hated that and that was why it was important for his strength and power to be heard. He needed to be recognized for the strong horse that he was, and these throwaway remarks were actually wounding him and causing part of the problem.

I worked very hard with Goldie. This poor horse had been through a lot – overworking, separation from a mare and foal he felt were 'his', moving to another country, difficulties in training. It all added up to quite a traumatic time. I was delighted to see that the hard work had paid off, though, when I got Audrey's next email: 'It was incredible to gain such amazing insights about Goldie (and myself) through your work. I am so excited. I must tell you that there has been a massive change in him since you have been treating and talking with him! My daughter rode him a few days ago with no problems and jumped a course of three jumps with him wearing only a halter and saddle. Then I rode him, and he was perfect. After I mounted up, he turned his head sideways and checked me out! Then we showed him his bridle, and he allowed us to put it on easily, when he could have walked away if he'd wanted to – we were in an arena and he was not restrained. We are absolutely delighted. We're yet to ride him in the bridle but I'm not anticipating any problems – we will build up the work gradually again. We all know that we have to work to communicate more effectively with him, and are prepared to do that.'

When a guardian is so loving and willing to take everything on board, it really does make my work worthwhile.

What was really interesting about Goldie was the issue of him being called 'gay'. The words we use are very important and animals react to them and the sense in which we use them. They can often see beneath the surface of what people present, as did Merlin the whippet-crossbreed who was horrified by me asking if he was a rescue dog. Because I work with so many rescue animals I have learned through time and experience that I get a particular feeling from them that is exclusive to rescue cases – this lets me know that I'm working with a rescue animal without having to ask them that specific question. However, I worked with Merlin before I reached that evolved stage of my communication journey and was still in the place where I always checked out this feeling by asking the animal if they had been rescued. Merlin's response stunned me. *No! No, I am not a rescue dog!* he shouted. I quickly changed tack and asked him how he met his mum.

He sent me an image of what looked like mucky grass (I presumed that it was a park) and I had the association of a walk but the feeling was definitely one of meeting. What was most interesting was that the focus wasn't actually the park or the walk or even the meeting, but a discussion. He then showed me a room where his mum was talking with other adults. This talking was very much about him. It was even clearer to me then that he *was* a rescue dog – he just didn't recognize it. But why? I asked him what was happening at the meeting. *I was just waiting for a new guardian. Someone who needed to be rescued. I was waiting for her.* Merlin clearly did not see himself as the rescue dog: from his perspective, *he* was waiting to rescue *her*. This was very important to him, because in his mind he did not need rescuing, she did – and he had done that for *her*.

This taught me so much. I always thought I was sensitive and tactful in my work with both people and animals, and had spent my working life dealing with other people's sensitive issues, but I cringe when I look back at early communication reports and see how, just as with Merlin, my line of questioning was clumsy and insensitive but most of all lacked the acknowledgement and appreciation that the animals have their own, valid, perspective on things.

Chapter 27

Making Sense of the Mental Chatter

Sometimes I will hear words clearly and I will have a conversation, but I hear these things in my own voice – though I know they're not my thoughts or words. I know that must sound rather confusing. Many think it's a sort of disembodied feeling but I'm afraid that isn't accurate either. I think the best way for me to describe it is as 'mental chatter'.

I sometimes get attitude with the voice of the animal as well. Although I'm hearing the words in my voice, I will sometimes have a sense of an attitude with it that isn't mine: maybe sarcasm or anger or sometimes, especially with cats, a real hoity-toity attitude. My back end will go and I'll feel the cat's tail swishing. My head and neck will elongate and the words might be along the lines of, *Huh, you're such a nuisance*, almost as if it just can't be bothered. Because I've been doing it for a while, I now know to trust this as genuine communication, but when I was first learning, when it was first happening to me, there was always the sense of *Is it just me creating these words?* So I'd ask guardians to give me specific questions so that they, and I, could verify the information I was receiving. I don't need to do that any more.

It's not the same as having a dialogue with somebody else; the information that is given back to me often provides answers with pictures or feelings, as I've illustrated. My work when tracking missing animals can be quite specific in terms of where they are lost, or where they have been picked up by someone else, and they can give quite clear descriptions of a new home or area or they can give me images of street names. Quite often I'll say to them, *If you're out walking, look for a street sign and send it to me.* It would be great if you could say, *Show me an envelope with an address* – and receive it every time! On one occasion I used that technique with a cat who was desperate to find its guardian and was locked in a house and couldn't get out. All I got was the house number that time but that and the area description brought about a happy ending.

There have been times when a lot of information has come through at once using different methods. One lady at a workshop gave me a picture of a horse, but no other information. I knew immediately that he had crossed the rainbow bridge and asked him about his passing. He showed me the most beautiful moving image, not a still, of him running through a field. The grass was so green that it was overly bright, like a cartoon colour, and the wind was flying through his mane. He said that he liked to jump, he hadn't been able to do it often but he could now, so I fed it all back. The woman was in tears. She said that she had been with him when he passed and that she'd been trying to communicate with him. She had told him, *When you're ready to go, send me an image of you running through a field of the brightest green grass,* and that's when she knew it was time to call the vet and have him put down. They had already set that up between themselves and now I was getting it – that totally blew me away. She loved him and was comforted by the reading, that I'd got the imagery of his passing over perfectly correct. A lot of people just want a sense of how their animals are if they've passed over, rather than specifics; they may want to apologize, ask if they'd done the right thing by letting them go, check they're OK, or just have some connection, but the animal almost always has so much more to offer in return.

Some of my best results come from horses, even though they scare me when I'm beside them. As a result of a chance meeting a woman called Nicola I ended up working on a horse yard with a lot of horses. We got chatting in a hairdresser's. She had no photograph; she just started telling me that she had bought a horse, Tristan, who cost a lot as an investment for her yard, but she couldn't work him. It was a complete waste of money and she didn't know what was wrong with him. As she put it, 'I can't do a dashed thing with him.' There were no photographs or anything, but, WHAM! As she spoke, he was there. I said, 'Your horse has been shunted.' That wasn't even a word I knew until that moment, and I certainly didn't know what it applied to. This all happened in a hairdresser's, where we had just started chatting! Something was hurting at the back end of Tristan – she just looked at me and said she had always suspected that the horse had been used for carriage driving and had been injured by the carriage, without the sellers telling her. Tristan wouldn't let anyone near his back end at all – he was really flighty – so I said I'd go out to the yard and work with him. I did and she asked me to look at another horse too. I did therapy work, and I stood as close as I felt comfortable – which wasn't that close, to be honest.

The healing and therapy worked well with Tristan and through that yard I learned a lot about how I would deal with horses. If the horse is OK with me touching their head and shoulders I will, but I don't need to for anything to work. I ask for them to be tied up outside so I can work around them. I have worked with horses in stables but I can feel quite anxious in that environment in case I get squashed into a corner. Also, when I get carried away and am lost in the healing work I'm not paying attention to the horse's behaviour, so, I always ask for the guardian to be present and my instructions to them are to look out for signs that he's likely to stand on my toes, for one thing. If I have my eyes closed and I'm concentrating particularly hard on getting one area of the body energized, I don't want to be trampled underfoot for my trouble! When a dog's had enough it'll wander away but that isn't going to happen in this situation, so the guardian has to help out.

Nicola had another horse, called Beauty, with whom I communicated too. I told her that I didn't know anything about horses but that the pain was *'right there'* – I just pointed and said that that was where he had difficulty moving – but that I also felt there was something coming in from '*here*', and again I showed her physically. I said, 'I really must get a book and learn horses' body parts,' but Nicola was horrified and, like the prevous yard owner, said the fact that I didn't know what things were called meant that she felt she was getting pure information from me. That for her was a bonus.

Somebody once asked me to ask their horse very specific questions and I didn't understand any of them. They asked if she wanted AI or a natural covering – this turned out to be a choice between having artificial insemination or bringing the stallion in! I had no idea – I never even knew that they had to show the stallion what to do in order to mate. There have been numerous situations with horses where things haven't meant anything to me and all I can do is to describe them as best as I can for the guardian.

At the start of my animal communication work, all of this was a speedy learning curve for me and the amount of cases I worked on gave me a swift insight into how some animals worked. Cats and dogs are so very different from each other: if you ask a cat who killed the mouse, you'll get, *It was me, me, me*; if you ask a dog who stole the chicken, you'll get, *Well, it wasn't me*.

Through experience and practice, both my therapy work and my animal communication work have developed and evolved over the years, allowing me to work much more quickly and efficiently. How I practise now is significantly different to when I started. While I have always carried out two communication sessions for each animal, initially I did this to build my confidence, using the second session to double-check information and use the guardians' initial feedback to shape the session. I no longer need that second session for checking out information, so now use the second session to work directly with the guardian and the animal together, creating a three-way communication flow – sending messages direct from one to the other.

As my work has evolved in this way, I'm being drawn more and more to identifying and supporting the healing of the guardians. I recently got a call from a woman who had a terribly behaved and nervous beagle. I appreciated all that she was telling me about it being difficult to discipline her dog, and the fact that he wouldn't adhere to house rules, but as soon as I tuned in I realized that the problems were hers, not his. This woman was in a relationship where her husband of many years was very controlling. All of her children had left home and she was pouring all of her love into her dog, to the extent that he constantly received mixed messages. She'd encourage him on to her lap when they were alone, then discourage him when her husband was around and made critical comments. She'd feed him scraps from the table when on her own, but punish him for begging when anyone else was there.

The poor dog didn't know if he was coming or going, and she was constantly projecting her own anxiety on to him. I gently tried to make some of these points, but it was a hopeless case as the relationship with her husband was key to finding a solution to the problems. If she hadn't suffered years of nervousness at his hands, she wouldn't be pouring her life and worries into her dog – but how could I fix all of that? She wanted to continue with more sessions for her dog, but, ethically, I had to refuse because I knew I could do nothing more to help the dog until she helped herself.

I got quite frustrated. That dog had huge stress and anxiety problems and they were completely created by his guardian. He told me that it was all about her and that he didn't have the capability of being the top dog in the house, which was the role she wanted him to take with her other animals, to whom she wasn't as close. When I put that to her she got very upset and said that she was aware that she was the root of the problems but didn't know how, or if she was able, to change. She needs to reach her own decisions in her own way in her own time. And I'll still be here waiting for her and Sweep when she does.

I'd worked on four cats for one of my clients, and one of them told me about the really stressful time the guardian was going through. The cat said her mum was the one who needed healing so I sent her healing energies, after seeing boots and suits and briefcases in the picture the cat sent me. There was clearly something to do with courts and it turned out she was involved in a big legal case. The cat didn't want healing, he wanted *his mum* to have it – she said she couldn't believe it when I told her what I'd done, because at the time of day I'd sent it she'd felt so much more positive and uplifted about the case.

Sometimes, I even forget what I can do. There was one situation when my friend and I were driving back from an early-morning run and found a sheep standing in the middle of the road. 'Slow down, Nicky,' I said, 'we'll need to try to get that sheep back into the field.' We did slow the car down and, as was to be expected, the sheep took flight when we got out. We could clearly see which field it had come from, as it was now at the fence looking earnestly at his friends, but we had absolutely no idea how it had got out – there were no holes or gaps anywhere. Nicky tried to create a space in the fence while I tried to herd it back. It was futile: the sheep wasn't going to go anywhere near Nicky and it took off up the road in the opposite direction. We were both really worried because we knew it wouldn't be long before the traffic would start to build on the road. Nicky said, 'Can you not do your communication thing?' I had been so worried about the sheep that I hadn't even considered that! Because I was stressed for the sheep I didn't know how effective communication would be, so I stood in the middle of the road facing the way the sheep had gone and closed my eyes to try to centre and ground myself. Goodness only knows what I looked like.

I sent a moving image to the sheep, showing him that if he turned around and walked back down the hill we would open the gate so he could walk through and join his friends. I promised him that we would stay well away and then sent him wonderful feelings of reunion and joy with the image of him being back in the field with his friends.

'Sarah-Jane, look!' Nicky called. I opened my eyes and there was the sheep slowly trotting back down the middle of the road straight towards me. I couldn't believe it. Nicky quickly opened the gate and we moved well out of the way. The sheep went straight to the gate and did a quick hop and ran straight through. How amazing – and how daft of me to not even consider doing what I spend every day doing.

Chapter 28

Full Circle

I was delighted when Kairyn, Dan's mum, got in touch with me about one of her other dogs, Rosco. However, it was rather a sad story. Rosco was old and Kairyn was in tears after returning from the vet's where she had been told he had suffered a stroke. Rosco was due to go back the next day to be put to sleep. She was devastated. She loved Rosco so much and wanted me to communicate with him and check out if there was anything else they could do for him. I was under a huge amount of pressure with this one and felt that I had come full circle since my early encounter with her dog Dan.

My initial impression from the photograph was that Rosco was a grumpy old man and the last thing he wanted to do was go to the vet. When I asked him why he was so against it, he told me, *It will do no good*. I felt there was a huge amount of fear attached to the impending visit and that he absolutely did not want to be put to sleep. This wasn't necessarily obvious, because some animals will accept that they are at the end of their time with us and will make plans to pass over. Rosco did not feel as if he was arguing against that; it was more that he was firmly against the vet being involved. I asked whether his time here with us on earth was coming to a close, and he said, *Yes*. I asked whether he was ready to leave his physical body, and again he said, *Yes*. However, when I asked whether he was ready to leave now, I got a firm, *No*. Similarly, when I asked whether his departure was imminent, he told me, *No, I'm holding on for my mum – she's not ready yet*. I asked whether he would like me to speak to her about this, but again he said, *No, don't rush, she needs time*. I wondered whether he needed permission from Kairyn to pass and he said, *Yes, but I'll know when she's ready*.

In view of Rosco's age and the fact that he was being put to sleep the following day, I felt it was imperative that I did a full body scan, checking every area of his body. When I asked whether he had any pain he sent me red flashes at his head area, which felt to be more on the right side. I also had a feeling of the head leaning or falling to the side. When I enquired whether he needed help with the pain, clever old Rosco sent me an image of half an aspirin tablet – he needed pain relief for his head. At this point in the communication I was drawn to his hindquarters. It felt as if they were stiff and the word *crumbly* came into my head. I also felt specifically that the liver was not good and that this needed to be checked out as well as the stomach.

Rosco, I said, *is there anything you would like me to tell your mum?* He wanted me to say to Kairyn that he loved her so much and that he was sorry for being such a burden. We had a long discussion about this. He was concerned that he tied his mum down and limited her life. I reassured him that when she took him on it was for the long haul and the very fact that we were communicating meant that she would always want the very best for him. More importantly, I had the very strong feeling that he wanted her to have a fuller life. I sensed that there was a restriction for her – as if her desires were being suffocated. Rosco's focus was really on Kairyn and his desire that she lead a full life when he left.

Then came the million-dollar question.

Have you suffered a stroke, Rosco? I asked.

No. No, I have not, but the headaches are blinding.

Goodness.

I checked again with him but he was adamant that he had not suffered a stroke. He said that he was happy in general, although rather sad at times that he was no longer the dog he once was, and that he was very, very tired. He said that he needed time and also sent me an image of him being stroked, comfortingly. I felt that he couldn't be bothered with the other dogs and that he needed time with a man he showed me. He sent me an image of him and this man snuggled up on the sofa. The image was accompanied by a feeling that this was not a usual occurrence.

His body scan told me that there was much physically wrong with Rosco – it was like a shopping list of ailments: his left front leg was tired and uncomfortable on stony ground; his bark was croaky; his right hip was creaky and I also saw flashes of red around the right eye and head, which is usually indicative of pain or inflammation; his right eye didn't feel good on the peripheral vision, as if it was blocked; there was pain along his lower back; neither ear felt as though the hearing was that great and the right side felt worse; his throat was dry and his lungs felt affected by smoke. He showed that there were side effects to the medication he was on, and he sent me *headaches* again, *blinding headaches*. Poor, poor Rosco.

The two chakras in the head area were full of excess energy, which explained his bad headaches. I worked on this area in particular, dispersing and grounding the energy as much as possible. Interestingly the throat chakra was blocked which would also contribute to a build-up around the head. The blocked throat chakra tied in with the croaky bark picked up on the body scan – and I thought that there could be an issue here with communication. Rosco's root chakra was also deficient of energy, which explained his hindquarters being tired and stiff. The lower chakras look after, among other things, the digestion, liver, kidneys, bladder and bowel. Because all of these chakras were deficient of energy I suspected that some of these essential body functions were under-performing.

The next day, Kairyn told the vet that she'd had animal-communication work done with Rosco and detailed my physical findings to her. This vet was wonderful and carefully worked her way around Rosco, checking out all the areas that I'd found to be causing him problems. The vet totally agreed with the stomach and liver issues I had highlighted and felt they were indeed the result of side effects of his medication. The issue with the lungs and breathing was also verified, as Rosco had smoke in the lungs after being on holiday with a heavy smoker. But, most interestingly, when she checked the eye, she found a build-up of pressure behind it, which was causing his headaches. In turn the pain was causing him to drop his head to the side. Not a stroke, but pressure behind the eye!

The terminology Rosco used turned out to be highly important: *blinding headaches* – the issue was his eye after all. Rosco did not need to be put to sleep and a happy mum and dog returned home to spend lots of one-to-one time together.

This was such a demanding and life-changing communication – Rosco's future had been in my hands, and yet again I felt so thankful that one of Kairyn's dogs had trusted me.

Anyone who communicates with animals must learn to trust the information they receive. We all have an internal critic – use yours to your advantage to push yourself to work harder, question more and hone your skills, but not to doubt yourself and your abilities. As I've already said, information will never be wrong but your *interpretation* of it may be.

I do have tips for everyone who is drawn to this work

and I really do hope that you use them to give you a head start to becoming your very own whisperer. When asking a question, delve deeper with each response – it's like peeling back an onion and there might be many layers before you get to the core. Keep a record of your successes and achievements to keep you strong when you have doubts. Even the best communicators get blocks – take time off and come back to it later. I want you to be excited about your communication success but if it inflates your ego it will get in the way of your ability to communicate, so stay grounded. Practise on other people's animals to build your skills and confidence – it's so much easier than communicating with your own, where you are emotionally involved and have a vested interest in the outcome. Practise, practise, practise – and then practise some more!

We can receive information through words, images, feelings and thoughts. All of it is valid and I believe we should view animal communication in the same way as learning a new language – as another animal communicator once said, you wouldn't expect to be able to speak fluent Spanish after two evening classes, would you? Take your time with this, and enjoy it.

Sometimes the animal can express quite explicitly what they want – as the communication practitioner you must then pass that on to the guardian and accept that your role is over. That can be hard and frustrating if the animal has been clear about what they need but the guardian is unwilling to action it. Your role, like mine, is to advocate on behalf of the animal and support them by speaking freely about what they tell you.

And what about the hard times? As clairsentience has always been my strongest psychic tool, I'm used to feeling the often overwhelming impact of an animal's heartfelt emotion – whether it is pain, trauma, anxiety, joy, happiness or sheer ecstasy. I always feel the emotion as if it's my own and will often find myself smiling or grinning – knowing it is the animal who is doing so. This happens a lot when talking to the guardian on the phone about their companion, especially if they ask a question. I often find myself grinning from ear to ear before they have even finished – that is their animal companion affirming the answer before the guardian has even finished asking the question.

I also feel painful or traumatic experiences as if they are my own. I feel the pain and hurt and can now gauge quite effectively how deep that pain and hurt is. Of course everyone's emotional pain is relative and that's how I gauge it too – I measure the depth of the pain that I feel and do not judge or mark the pain against the incident. For example, for most animals the loss of a loved one is deep and lasting, but I know from the depth of the pain that I feel how easily it could be cleared with a little therapy work. For some, however, I know the depth of the pain is such that it is preventing the animal from moving on and, in some extreme cases, a trauma is so painful that they are protecting themselves from further hurt and pain by shutting down and closing themselves off emotionally. This level of pain is much more deep-rooted and sometimes requires fairly intensive work to clear. However, just like us, some animals have a hugely deep traumatic reaction to a situation that others could cope with relatively easily. My job is not to judge but to feel, so that I can be in the animal's shoes and understand exactly how they are feeling.

People are often surprised that I can work with such deeply felt emotions and pain and I am often asked, 'How do you do it? I couldn't bear it.' I do it because it's the only way the animal can express and therefore release that pain. That is my job: to hear what is going on and to hold that space for the animal to just be. To feel the pain allows me to understand, and to be able to convey to the guardian just how deeply felt the emotion is. This creates the right starting position for all three of us to begin exploring positive solutions for the animal and, where appropriate, for the guardian too.

So, do I spend my days crying in my treatment room? No. That's not how it works for me. Yes, I feel it and, yes, I feel tears, but I know they are not mine – they belong to the animals. Because of this, the tears (with the exceptions of Bluey and Dolly) never actually fall. That's not my job. How helpful or professional would it be if you went to the GP and he cried when you told him a close family member had died, or wept uncontrollably when telling you that you had cancer? This is my job, my profession, where my role is to support and always remember that I am merely a tool to help animals to express what they need to express. These are their emotions, not mine. I'm just the transmitter. I don't need to take them on and hold them – that would make me no good to anyone. Carrying around everyone else's emotions and traumas? It wouldn't be long before I wouldn't be able to work.

Epilogue

The End is Just the Beginning

Animal communication is a mind-to-mind connection established from a heart-to-heart connection.

I began my life terrified of animals, yet now I spend my days talking to them and I absolutely love it. Horses, dogs, cats, guinea pigs, birds, camels, dingoes, donkeys, dolphins – you name them, I've had a conversation with them!

As a pet whisperer, I have been privileged to find something I want to spend the rest of my days doing and I couldn't even begin to imagine how I would feel if this wondrous world was no longer open to me. This is the life that was marked out for me and I sometimes feel like the luckiest woman in the world, because the animals never gave up on me, and never took 'no' for an answer, though I was a far from willing participant when it all began. In fact, I fought tooth and nail to deny that this was my calling. Thankfully, there was something bigger than me – some greater power – that kept returning and finally opened my eyes to what my place is in the circle of life.

And that power did so through a dog called Dan and

all the wonderful creatures who followed him. It's not a traditional career but I'm blessed to have it. If I can do this work, anyone can. People may feel silly or think that they'll not be able to communicate with animals, but you just need to be open. As a child, if I saw a dog I'd scream for my mum. The fear made me not like them very much, which makes it even more remarkable that I can do this so, if you already have a connection and love of animals, you are miles ahead of where I started! Some people were born talking to animals, while others had to learn how to rekindle their deeply buried abilities. I'm part of that latter group and I can teach you how to do it too.

It has been an exciting and exhilarating journey but it's been lonely, isolating, frustrating and scary too. Remember that it began with random dogs popping into my mind and the thought that I was going mad. It felt like a high-speed car ride over which I had no control – but I completely trusted that I would arrive safely at my destination and I have.

My message to you is simple. Be inspired. Inspired by my story, inspired by the thought of change and, most of all, inspired by your own devotion and love of animals. I encourage you to be inspired to take it further – to reach out and communicate and heal, lovingly and deeply, just like I do. *Because you can*. After all, if I, as someone who has spent their life terrified of animals, can reach out and connect with them, love them and heal them, then I believe that anyone who already loves animals can take that love, fine-tune it and start communicating with our animal companions on a newer, deeper, more intimate level.

I believe we are all born with the ability to reach out and intuitively connect with animals – we already do this with people that we love and care about. Communicating with animals is merely taking our natural intuition to the next level – doing it consciously, with intent.

These closing paragraphs are, in some ways, the hardest to write. How can I end something which is only just beginning? The chapters may have come to a close, but there will be so many more stories for me to tell. My words barely express the many beautiful ways in which I have been touched by all that has happened to me, but I hope I have managed to reach out to each and every one of you by sharing my incredible story.

This is my amazing world and I warmly invite you and your beloved animals to join me in the next stage of this magical journey . . .

Want to learn how to talk to animals?

As someone who grew up terrified of animals but who now has the joy and privilage of speaking to and healing them on a daily basis, Sarah-Jane has a passion and commitment to teach others how to ignite their own innate ability to communicate with animals.

Sarah-Jane's belief is simple: *if she can learn how to communicate with animals then **anyone** can!* If you already love animals and want to make a positive difference in their lives, then go along to one of Sarah-Jane's relaxed and interactive workshops, where you will discover how to connect with your animal guide and learn all you need to know to communicate with animals – and have fun practising on the day!

For more information on Animal Communication or Animal Healing Workshops please go to:

www.soul2soultherapy.co.uk or phone +44 (0)1592 787867